Concordancing and Corpus Analysis Using MP 2.2

Michael Barlow

ATHELSTAN

Requirements:
Windows OS
Disk space: 1.5 MB
RAM: 32MB

Related products:
ParaConc
WordSkew
Collocate
Concordances in the Classroom. 1997. C. Tribble and G. Jones
Learning with Corpora. 2001. Guy Aston (ed.).

info@athel.com
www.athel.com

Athelstan
2429 Bissonnet, Ste 464
Houston, TX 77005
U.S.A.

Preface

Since language is a fundamental component of human society, it is not surprising that investigations of language in general, as well as the language of particular texts, are of interest to a wide range of "researchers," from psychologists to lawyers to students learning a second language. Traditionally, the main sources of information about the structure and use of language have been standard reference texts such as dictionaries and grammars. These sources undoubtedly have their uses and will continue to do so, especially those reference works based on corpus analysis, but they do not provide direct access to instances of language use. There is, for example, no dictionary of computer chat-room language, no grammar of the language of prefaces or corporate web-pages, nor are there published wordlists for written business German. Consequently, in order to investigate the nature of specific texts, the best approach is to collect an appropriate corpus and analyse it, perhaps making use of general reference works as a point of departure.

context of *sin* Many years ago in the days before computers and even before commercial printing, scholars found it instructive to (manually) produce a concordance of an important work such as the Bible so that each occurrence of a word such as *begat* or *sin* could be grouped with all the other instances of the word, along with their context of use. There was, and is, much that can be gained from breaking up the rhetorical, logical structure of a text to reveal and analyse the repetitive lexical and phrasal language patterns that lie hidden in a linear discourse.

Today, data-driven, usage-based and corpus-based approaches are popular in language teaching, linguistic research, and natural language processing. Underlying these different methodologies is an emphasis on finding and exploiting the patterns and structures inherent in text data, which can be revealed by powerful text analysis tools. *MP 2.2*, described here, is a full-featured text-searching program that is complex enough to offer considerable power and flexibility, while being simple enough to allow a corpus to be loaded and searched in a few seconds (as described on page 14). This version of the program provides, in addition to simple text searches, the full power of Regular Expressions and also includes a Part-of-

Speech Tag search. These and other features, such as advanced sort and advanced collocation options, provide the researcher with extensive control over the format of search queries along with the tools necessary to analyse complex texts containing mark-up, part-of-speech tags, or html code. The very latest version, 2.2, allows for the comparison of corpus word lists and contains commands to extract and show collocations.

Naming

MonoConc Pro, it has to be admitted, is not the best name in the world. It sounds rather harsh and seems, even to me, as though it might refer to something growing in a petri dish. It is, in fact, a derivative of the name of another software program, *ParaConc*. This predecessor program (in terms of naming) is a concordancer for use with parallel (i.e., translated) texts.

The *Pro* part of the name, which should be taken with a large pinch of irony, distinguishes *MonoConc Pro* from *MonoConc 1.5*—a simpler and more restricted concordance program. In what follows, we will follow the example of companies such as British Petroleum (BP) and Imperial Chemical Industries (ICI) and seek cover in the form of initials and use the name *MP 2.2*.

Updates

Updates to this guide and news related to MP2.2 are available on the website: www.monoconc.com.

Contents

1. Introduction

In this first chapter, we introduce the notion of text analysis, give some mundane details on installing *MP* 2.2, and step through a simple search in order to get a sense of the basic commands and the flow of the software.

1.1 Text Analysis

MP 2.2 is a sophisticated concordance package, which doubtless has more uses than one person can imagine, but essentially it allows a corpus (i.e., one or more text-only files) to be analysed to reveal formal patterns, particularly those which cannot be perceived easily in the linear stream of written or spoken text. Obvious examples of hidden information that can be brought to light using a text-analysis program are a list of the most common words occurring in a text, or the words that only occur once (*hapax legomena*), or, somewhat less obviously, the most common sentence-initial words.

The usefulness of the program lies in helping the user to investigate language-related information in a corpus, based on the use of different queries or searches. The kinds of information that can be extracted depend on the format of the corpus, as discussed in detail below. It is also true to say that the information derived from the corpus depends on the ingenuity, and, to some extent, the patience of the concordance user. In the past—even in the recent past—some readers may have looked for key examples by reading a novel and underlining the features of interest. These methods are not only very laborious, but there always remains a doubt about the accuracy of the results obtained in this way, and double-checking this kind of data is too onerous to even contemplate.

A concordance program can search for patterns in a text very easily and very quickly. In addition, the ability to sort the concordance lines takes us beyond the mere collection of examples and allows the visual identification of common patterns. Repeated occurrences of a text pattern naturally stand out, and the more frequent a pattern, the more it stands out, which means that much can be revealed by simply scanning fairly rapidly through sorted concordance lines.

In the concordance results window, the search word is centred, as shown in Figure 1.

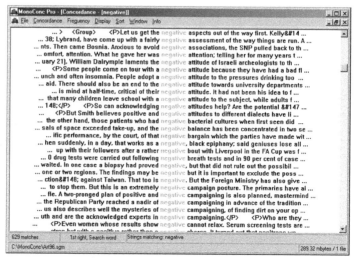

Figure 1. Concordance lines (sorted)

Centring the keyword gives concordance lines their characteristic shape. It has the advantage of making it very easy to identify the location of the search term and it also means that sorting the lines creates a visual patterning that makes recurrent patterns stand out.

annotation

Some texts contain annotations or mark-up such as *<head> England Collapse </head>* or *talk_VB*. Other texts contain little or no mark-up, in which case the data extracted will be based solely on the characters or words in the text itself. For example, we can find out what words in English end in the letters *dous*. I am not sure why you would want to know, but if you did, then you could discover that there are only four such words: *hazardous, horrendous, stupendous,* and *tremendous* (and perhaps *Aldous*). Alternatively, you could investigate the VERB + *my way* construction and observe that in a newspaper corpus the common "way" verbs are *make, find, work* and *lose*, with rarer verbs such as *fumble, munch* and *wangle* also showing up.

*dous

The *-dous* and VERB + *my way* searches have to be specified in different ways. Searching for all words ending in *dous* is accomplished very easily by employing a simple text search for ***dous**, where * represents zero or more characters occurring in the word before the *dous* ending. In contrast, the search for the *way* construction in an untagged text involves more effort in searching for and extracting the relevant patterns since in a text with no mark-up the user cannot search for the category VERB. The information on the VERB + *way* construction given above had to be retrieved by searching for *my way* and then sorting

10

the concordance results in such a way that verbs immediately preceding *my way* could be identified and counted using the COLLOCATE FREQUENCY DATA command.

As I write these paragraphs, *MP 2.2* is running in the background, searching through 180 million words of newspaper texts to find if there are particular patterns associated with MAKE + PRONOUN + VERB versus LET + PRONOUN + VERB. The newspaper corpus is untagged and so the search query must include the different forms of *make* and all the different object pronouns in English. The first search reveals 14,246 instances of MAKE + PRONOUN and it turns out that common verbs filling the verb slot following the pronoun are *feel, look, seem and sound.* There are only 4,897 "hits" with *let* and the common verbs in this case are *know, go, get, have* and *do.* This quick search gives us some idea of the relative frequency of the *make* versus *let* causative constructions. Furthermore, by looking at the co-occurring verbs we see that the contrast is not simply one of *making someone do something* versus *letting someone do something*, but that in the newspaper texts the *make* causative often occurs with mental verbs such as *feel* and *seem*; whereas *let* seems to be more closely associated with direct action verbs, as in *let him go,* although *let him know* is also a common collocation. (More information on searching for syntax is given in Section 6.)

If the corpus is enhanced with mark-up or tags which explicitly identify particular aspects of the text, such as the part-of-speech (POS) of each word, or divisions such as headlines, bylines, etc., then searches can be constructed that make use of the mark-up, thereby making the investigation of causatives and other constructions much easier. As we will see below, there are different ways in which searches can refer to mark-up. Of course, the mark-up in a text can always be included as part of any string search, but as described in Section 5, POS tag information can conveniently be incorporated in searches via the use of a TAG SEARCH, which makes it much easier to work with tagged texts.

To give another example, if you want to know which words commonly occur in headlines, you can carry out a context search that locates just those words that appear between the tags *<head>* and *</head>*. If you do this for text from a broadsheet newspaper, you will discover that the words typically found include: *chief, crime, home, inquiry, move, murder, news, offer, over, plan, record, rise, says, seeks, start, step, success, support, talks, time, warning,* and *world.* Naturally, analysing the content of headlines in tabloid or business newspapers will yield a rather different set of words.

But we are getting ahead of ourselves here. Let's start at the beginning.

11

1.2 Installation

copy files

MP 2.2 can be installed by copying all the files on the CD-ROM (or downloaded folder) to your computer. In most cases, the first step is to make a directory called MP and then simply copy the files to that directory. (*MP 2.2* does not come with an installation utility, and if you are unsure how to copy files, you should refer to your Windows manual.)

It is a good idea to create four subdirectories within your MP directory: Texts (for different corpora), Workspaces (for workspace files), Results (for saved concordance and frequency information) and Loads (for stop lists and complex searches).

For the program to function, the only file that actually needs to be transferred to your hard drive is **MP2.2.exe**, which is around one megabyte in size. The help file, **MP2.2.hlp** and the help contents file **MP2.2.cnt** should also be copied to the hard disk. These three files constitute the software program. If desired, the sample text files on the MonoConc Text disk, which include Jane Austen's *Northanger Abbey* and three files containing transcripts from White House press conferences, can also be copied to the hard disk. The files containing the transcripts constitute the demo texts. These texts are themselves not necessary for the program to function, but needless to say *some* text file has to be loaded.

The commercial corpora used in the following sections are the Meetings sub-corpus of the *Corpus of Spoken Professional American English* (available from Athelstan) and the tagged *BNC Sampler Corpus* (available from the British National Corpus; see http://info.ox.ac.uk/bnc).

1.3 Requirements

1.3.1 Disk space

As noted above, the software files constituting *MP 2.2* require a a megabyte or so of disk space on a hard disk drive. In the course of its operation, *MP 2.2* also writes some small, temporary files to disk and creates or updates an **ini** file, which stores information such as settings and the search query histories. *MP 2.2* also allows the user to save a workspace, that is, to save the current corpus links and other settings. This workspace is saved as a file, which is typically around 10K in size, but the associated workspace folder may be anything from 2-20MB or more, depending on the extent of the tags, etc.

1.3.2 Compatible versions of Windows

MP 2.2 is a 32-bit program and hence must be run under Windows 95 or higher. Any higher Windows versions, including Windows XP, System 7 etc are acceptable platforms. The software should also run under 64-bit Wiindows. *MP 2.2* is not optimised for any particular system and is designed to run under a wide range of hardware/software configurations.

1.3.3 RAM

It is recommended that a computer with Windows 95 installed have 16 MB of RAM and a Windows XP system should have a minimum of 32 MB of RAM. As always, the more RAM the better, but it is possible to run the program with minimal configurations; the program is designed to work with whatever memory is available.

1.4. Starting *MP 2.2*

To start the program, double-click on the file *MP2.2*. Once the program is open, a simple screen appears, as shown below in Figure 2. This initial screen looks rather bare, containing only a blank window and two menu items: FILE and INFO.

Figure 2: Initial screen

Note that the information field in the lower left corner states: "No files loaded."

13

1.4.1 A quick look at *MP 2.2*

sample search A very important aspect of the design of *MP 2.2* is the ease and speed with which a search can be carried out. To illustrate this and to get an overall sense of the operation of *MP 2.2*, you can follow the instructions below to perform a quick text search. If you would rather follow a more methodical, step-by-step introduction, then ignore this diversion and move directly to the next part of this section on page 16.

1. Choose LOAD CORPUS FILE(S) from the FILE menu.

2. Select one or more text files.

3. When the files are being loaded, click on Cancel All in the COLLECTING TAG INFO dialogue box. (If the corpus is small, you may not see this dialogue box—or will see it perhaps only as a flash or two.)

4. Choose SEARCH from the CONCORDANCE menu.

5. Enter a search string (a word or phrase) and click OK (or press return).

6. Press Enter (or click Cancel) if you wish to halt the search.

7. Examine the results in the concordance window. The hits will be easier to view if you maximise the window.

8. Try sorting the concordance lines, using commands in the SORT menu to look for different patterns in the data.

9. Look at the simple collocate frequency data by choosing COLLOCATE FREQUENCY DATA from the FREQUENCY menu.

10. If the concordance results window is not visible, you can use the WINDOW menu to bring a selected window to the foreground.

1.4.1.1 Troubleshooting

no hits? If, contrary to your expectations, the search returned no finds or "hits," then it may be because the word or phrase you looked for is not present in the text. Words are much rarer than is commonly assumed, which means that your "favourite word" may just not be in the corpus. As a simple illustration of word frequencies, I arbitrarily chose the word *busybody* and searched for this word (with and without a hyphen) in a 180-million word newspaper corpus, which is equivalent to a few years' output of a daily newspaper. How many times would you expect the word *busybody* to occur in this large a corpus? It

14

turns out that in 180 million words there were only 50 instances, which is roughly one *busybody* per 4 million words. Looking for *busybodies*, I found, somewhat surprisingly, that there were 64 examples, more than the singular form. Overall, we see that *busybody* or *busybodies* shows up approximately once per 1.5 million words in a newspaper corpus. Given the rarity of words, it is obvious that combinations of words are going to be extremely rare. A search for *interfering busybody*, which seems like a very plausible-sounding phrase, produces just one exemplar in this large corpus. In other words, one possible reason for the lack of success in finding examples may be that the word you choose is much rarer than you had imagined and simply does not occur in the corpus that you are searching.

Assuming that the word or phrase does actually occur in the text, there are two common reasons for a failed search. One possibility arises from the fact that the simple text search is technically a word/phrase search rather than a string search. Thus searching for **tex** using the simple text search option will not locate *cortex* or *text*. To capture these forms, the search string must be formulated as ***tex***, or something similar. Adding such wildcards will permit words that are surrounded by other material to be located. Another common cause of surprising results relates to the specification of word delimiters—the characters such as space, tab, period, etc. that indicate a word boundary. If you search for the word *cortex* and the word occurs in the text with an attached tag, as in *<w NN>cortex*, then whether or not *cortex* is "found" depends on whether > is listed as a word delimiter in SEARCH OPTIONS. (By default > is a word delimiter, but this is changeable by the user.) If > is not in the list of word delimiters, then the search algorithm will treat the "word" as *<w NN>cortex* rather than *cortex* and thus once again, in order to capture this instance, we would have to use a wildcard search such as ***cortex**. (Delimiters are discussed in more detail in Section 9.)

If you found 500 instances of your search word, and this was fewer than expected, then the low number of hits found is likely to result from the setting of MAX SEARCH HITS in SEARCH OPTIONS. In *MP 2.2* the factory default for MAX SEARCH HITS is set to 500 hits, but the number of hits can be as high as required by the user. (There are always limits, of course, but these are very high; the upper limit of 16,000 hits in *MonoConc 1.0* does not apply in this version of the program.)

1.4.2 Specifying commands

commands

Before examining the functionality of the program in detail, we should first establish a protocol for the description of *MP2.2* commands. In this guide, the operation of the program is typically described in terms of commands issued via the mouse. This is partly for expository purposes; the phrase "select LOAD CORPUS FILE(S) from the FILE menu" is much clearer than "execute ALT-F L." In terms of actually using the software, learning some basic keyboard commands will make program operation a little faster and smoother. And if you prefer a keyboard style rather than a mouse style of issuing commands, then in reading through this text, you will be able to observe the keyboard equivalents of the mouse-based commands by paying attention to the following conventions. The menus and commands are displayed in the text with one letter underlined (as they are on the screen). For menus, this underlining indicates the "ALT letter" sequence that will select the menu. For instance, to select the FILE menu, enter ALT-F. In the case of commands, the underlined letter indicates the keyboard letter that will execute the command once the appropriate menu is selected. For example, to initiate a LOAD CORPUS FILE(S) command when the FILE menu is selected, enter L from the keyboard. Thus the complete keyboard command to load a text is ALT-F L. Since loading texts into the program is an important operation, a control sequence, CTRL-L, has also been assigned to this function. (Note: although the control character is standardly represented here in upper case form for clarity, the lower case version should actually be used—the command is CTRL plus lowercase l, not L.) Thus there are actually three ways in all to invoke this command: (i) using the mouse and selecting LOAD CORPUS FILE(S), (ii) entering the sequence ALT-F L, or (iii) entering the control command CTRL-L.

1.4.3 Back to the beginning

FILE and INFO   Let us return to the beginning and work through the different features methodically. Once the program is open, a simple screen appears which contains a blank window and two menus: FILE and INFO.

HELP   Let us deal with INFO first. This menu is always present; it provides access to HELP and to some basic information about *MP* 2.2, as well as some contact information for Athelstan. The HELP menu is organised according to topic (see Figure 3). Double-clicking on the appropriate heading will open the topic file, allowing perusal of the associated descriptions. In addition, the Windows Help utility provides other ways (such as FIND and INDEX) to locate the required information. Navigation of HELP is straightforward and will not be described here. (The two Help files, MP2.2.hlp and MP2.2.cnt, must be available in order for this information to be displayed.)

A further source of information is the brief description of each command when the command is selected. If you are not sure what action is associated with a particular menu item, you can move the pointer to the command (without clicking) and read the short description that appears in the lower left corner of the window. For example, if the cursor is on LOAD CORPUS FILE(S), the description that appears is "Add file(s) to current corpus," which is at least marginally more descriptive than the name of the command itself: Load Corpus File.

Figure 3: Help contents

Selecting the FILE menu reveals several commands, one of which is the now well-known LOAD CORPUS FILE(S) option, but before making a corpus available for searching we first need to take a look at a couple of other commands: LANGUAGE and TAG SETTINGS, which are described in the next chapter.

2. Working with a Corpus

2.1 What is a corpus?

As far as *MP* 2.2 is concerned, a corpus is any text-only file, or set of text-only files, that can be loaded into the program for analysis. However, the results of an analysis will only be interpretable and useful if the corpus has been created according to a reasonable set of crieria and if it is in keeping with the interests of the designer / analyst. In cases where the initial attempts to gather material for a corpus are indiscriminate and ad-hoc, then the results of corpus analysis will be meaningless. If one part of the corpus is a Jane Austen novel, one part is contemporary dialogue between close friends, and another part is a downloaded web-page of unknown origin, then it is difficult to see what we might say about the results of a search for a word or phrase. In other words, a corpus has to represent *something*. In practice, what a corpus represents depends to some extent on the particular perspective of the corpus analyst, which means, in effect, that there are numerous ways of constructing a corpus and numerous views on what a corpus represents. For instance, we might interpret a corpus in one or more of the following ways.

(i) an artefact (e.g., the writings of Jane Austen can be seen as one component of a cultural history)

(ii) a sample of a particular dialect or genre

(iii) a representation of a language

(iv) a representation of a speaker's productive knowledge

(v) the input to a language learner (child or second language learner)

(vi) the output of a speaker or particular group of speakers.

These perspectives may help you identify your own views on what the corpus you are working with represents.

The typical, perhaps implicit, assumption is that since a corpus is a sample of language, then it represents language in general in some manner. However, if you actually tied to pursue the goal of creating a corpus that represents language in a general way, you would soon come across some of the conceptual problems inherent in such an enterprise. Again, as an aid to thinking about the form of a corpus and how it relates to language in use, I have listed some different approaches to the representation of a language in order to help you choose which black hole you want to leap into.

(i) Identify the genres in a language and ensure that they are all represented in the corpus.

(ii) Identify the relative proportion of different genres within a language, then collect representative samples of each one, maintaining the appropriate proportions.

(iii) Identify different populations of language users (based on dimensions like age, gender, social class, L1, L2), then collect representative samples of the language that each user encounters.

(iv) Identify the different populations of language users, then collect samples of the language produced by each population.

(v) Identify the proportions of each type of language user with a community and the proportion of different genres used, and collect samples appropriately.

We don't need to consider these issues further here. Let us, instead, turn to and take heart from some successful exemplars of corpus construction.

2.2 Some models of corpus creation

The following brief descriptions of some different English corpora provide a selection of different approaches to corpus compilation. For more detailed descriptions, see the references given for each of the corpora.

2.2.1 Brown corpus

A major landmark in the creation of computer corpora is the Brown Corpus (Francis and Kucera 1964). This million-word corpus consists of 500 samples of approximately 2000 words each. The samples of written American were taken from a wide range of fiction and non-fiction text types, as described in Kennedy (1998:24-26). The choice between using samples or portions of texts versus whole texts is one parameter that distinguishes different kinds of corpora.

2.2.2. London-Lund Corpus

The half a million word London-Lund corpus is based on spoken British English used in academic settings in the 60s and early 70s. A portion of the corpus, showing the annotations marking phonological features, is illustrated below. To search such a corpus, it is necessary to make use of padding characters, as described in Section ?9.2.

2.2.3 COBUILD Bank of English

The ambitious COBUILD project, begun in 1980, was a cooperative project led by John Sinclair involving the commercial publisher Collins and members of the Department of English at Birmingham University. The corpus work was undertaken because the "two parties shared an interest in developing a new, thorough-going, description of the English language" (Renouf 1987:1). The aim was to identify those aspects of the English language revelant to the international use and so the guidelines for the samples used were as follows (Renouf 1987: 2)

-written and spoken modes
-broadly general rather than technical
-current usage, and preferably very recent
-naturally occurring text, not drama
-prose, including fiction; excluding poetry
-the language of adults (16+)
-'standard' English; no regional dialects
-predominantly British English, with some American, etc.

For a variety of reasons, the following proportions were used in compiling the corpus.

- book authorship: 75% male, 25% female
- dialect: 70% British, 20% American, 10% other
- mode: 75% written, 25% spoken

In selecting written texts, the compilers tried to identify widely read texts and hence they preferred to select bestsellers rather than sample texts randomly.

In 1990, Sinclair created a monitor corpus, the Bank of English, to which new material is constantly added (and some older material removed). The control of such large repositories of texts is subject to various difficulties associated with the size and the dynamic nature of the text materials being maintained.

2.2.4 British National Corpus

The British National Corpus (BNC) is now sometimes viewed as a historical corpus, representing British English from 1991-1995. The creation of the 100 million word corpus represents a major effort in design and implementation. It contains an SGML mark-up that conforms to the TEI (Text Encoding Initiative) Guidelines and the corpus includes part-of-speech tags (see Section 2.2.3.). Each text consists of a header and a body. The header contains information on the author of the text, the source of the text etc., and the body contains the text itself, or, strictly, a sample (of up to 40,000 words) of the text.

The selection of texts was based both on production (sampling texts from the range of materials being produced) and on reception (as judged by bestseller lists, library loan figures, etc.). The 4,124 texts in the BNC are divided into written (90%) and spoken (10%).

2.2.5 American National Corpus

The American National Corpus, which is loosely modelled on the BNC, is being compiled.

2.2.6 MICASE

The MICASE corpus (Simpson et al) contains transcriptions of a variety of spoken interactions on the University of Michigan campus, including advising sessions, large lectures, seminars, and other kinds of interactions. The header contains information such as the following:

Title: Medical Anthropology Lecture
Academic Division: Social Sciences and Education
RESTRICTIONS ON CITATION OF EXAMPLES: NONE
Recording Duration: 69 min.
Recording Date: February 25, 1998
Language: Primary Discourse Mode: MLG
Native Speaker
Participants: Number of Speakers: 5
Number of Students: 40
S1: Native-Speaker Status: Native speaker, American English; Academic Role: Junior Faculty; Gender: Female; Age: 31-50; Restriction: None
Setting: Large Classroom, Mason Hall

2.2.7. Helsinki Corpus

The Helsinki Corpus of English texts is a diachronic corpus of 1.5 million words covering Old English to Early Modern English (Kytö 1991, Kytö and Rissanen 1992). The texts in the corpus are coded according to 25 parameters, including the author's age and sex, date of the text, and dialect of the text, etc.

2.2.8 Corpus of Spoken American English (Santa Barbara Corpus)

Chafe, Dubois, and Thompson (1991) pointed out the need for a corpus of Spoken American based loosely on the model of the London-Lund corpus. The corpus contains dialogues from a variety of speakers of Standard American English in different settings.

2.2.9. ICLE

The International Corpus of Learner English is a cooperative corpus, which is added to as researchers in different countries compile corpora based the output of new groups of learners. The main features of a learner corpus with respect to the language dimension are medium, genre, topic, technicality, and task setting; and for the learner dimension: age, sex, mother tongue, religion, other foreign languages, level, learning context, and practical experience (Granger 1998:8). ICLE is constructed from argumentative, non-technical essays of approximately 500 words. Information on the learners comes from a questionnaire which they complete.

Astute readers will have noticed that all the corpora listed are based on English. And while more corpora have been developed for English than for other languages, there are a variety of non-English corpora available. Some of these consist of texts of cultural importance, but there are also contemporary corpora, some of which are based on spoken language. A variety of non-English corpora are available from the Linguistic Data Consortium and the TELRI project.

2.3 Settings for a particular corpus

Let us return to some mundane technical issues related to the loading of the files making up a corpus into *MP* 2.2.

Most corpora have some sort of annotation and it is usually beneficial to specify the form of annotations before initiating the loading of a corpus so that the file-loading process can take account of the mark-up format, allowing, for example, exclusion of tags in searches and word counts.

The following description might seem to be somewhat involved, but once the settings are entered, then the processing and display of the corpora and the search results will be much clearer. In addition, the use of "workspaces," which are described in the sSction 8, is a good way to ensure that the information about the annotations used in the corpus only has to be entered once.

Once the corpus files are selected and loaded, an automatic file-processing procedure is instigated. This COLLECT TAG INFORMATION routine will take some time to process a large corpus. On the other hand, with a small corpus, you may just about notice some flashes as each file is rapidly loaded and processed. To stop the processing of the text files, choose CANCEL ALL when the files are being loaded. Halting the file-processing is appropriate when you plan to do a simple search of a large corpus containing minimal annotations. The consequence of omitting this pre-processing is that the program will not be able to track tags or show the distribution of hits throughout the corpus. Some of the structure of the corpus files will be opaque to the program and it will not be able to distinguish the text itself from annotations of the text, but skipping this procedure does not affect the core functionality of the program.

COLLECT TAG INFORMATION can be invoked at any time, and it can also be run at the same time as other procedures such as searches.

MP 2.2 does not know anything about the special text formatting conventions of the different word-processing programs, and so files produced using a word-processor must be saved as text-only ANSI files, rather than as the regular file type (such as a Word or RTF document), which contain boldface and other formatting information tied to the particular word-processor. Whether or not the regular files actually contain formatting (boldface etc.), they must be saved as text-only files before they can be searched by the program.

It is a good idea to make a copy of your files before creating the text-only versions. The details of producing the correct kind of file can be found in the manual for your word-processing program under the heading of ANSI or text-only files.

gárblëd tèxt
If you are working with English texts, you can use ASCII files, but if you have non-English ASCII files containing accents, etc., then attempts to load them into *MP 2.2* will cause the accented characters to appear in garbled form. You must transform the files into ANSI text format by opening them using a Windows-based word-processor and then saving a copy of the files as Windows (ANSI) text. (There is a unicode versus of MonoConc – MP 2.3.)

2.3.1 Choosing a Language

Russian, Thai
The appropriate method of entering characters with accents and the definition of alphabetical (sorting) order depends on whether the current language is, for instance, English, Russian or Thai. Choosing LANGUAGE displays a list of languages, allowing the selection of the one appropriate for your corpus. (The range of languages displayed will depend on the version and configuration of Windows installed on your machine and on the choice of Regional Settings.) If the language you want is not present in the list, you should simply select the font that you want to use. For information on entering accented and other special characters, see Section 13.

24

If *MP* 2.2 is running under a system as different as, say, Chinese Windows, then the settings and behaviour will naturally be somewhat different from the description given here.

Warning:
If a language other than the current language is selected by choosing Okay (or hitting return) in the LANGUAGE dialogue box, then any loaded text files will be removed (unloaded). In other words, changing the language from English (United States) to English (United Kingdom) will cause the automatic unloading of the corpus, and so it is advisable to first select the language and then load the corpus.

2.3.2 Choosing a Font

Selecting the LANGUAGE command brings up a dialogue box which allows the font to be changed.

2.3 .3 Tag Settings and Collect Tag Information

More often than not, text files contain, in addition to the text or content itself, a set of tags or annotations or mark-up that provides extra explicit information about the the source of the text or about the components of the text, such as the division into title and body. In some cases the mark-up is minimal, as is the case with the demo text files included with *MP* 2.2. Most of these files are selections of spoken transcripts and include a single tag, which indicates the speaker's name, as shown here.

<SP>CLINTON:</SP> Well, I don't think it's useful to get into blame.

In this corpus there is a simple but very important distinction between the strings of letters and symbols that identify the speaker and the strings of letters that represent the words actually spoken. If this distinction is made in the text, then it is best if the program treats the text *per se* and the tags or mark-up as separate kinds of objects. There are some complexities involved here, which are discussed below, but to give a simple example it is clear that generally the calculation of frequency information should be based solely on the contents of the text should be used, not the words comprising the tags. (Note: if you wanted to include the words in tags, you could do it by purposely not indicating the structure of tags in TAG SETTINGS or by deselecting SKIP TAGS in FREQUENCY OPTIONS.)

Increasingly, corpora are highly tagged with information representing the source and structure of texts. The *BNC Sampler* CD-ROM, for example, contains texts that look like the following.

tagged corpus   <text decls="CN004 HN001 QN000 SN002" complete=Y org=COMPO>

<div1 n="08-NOV-89 edition, page " complete=Y org=SEQ>

<head type=MAIN>

<s n=0001 p=Y><w NP1>Lebanon<w NN1>leader <w VVZ>builds <w NN1>cabinet<c YSTP>. </s>

</head>

<head type=BYLINE>

<s n=0002 p=Y><w II>By <w NP1>Reuter <w II>in <w NP1>Beirut</s>

</head>

<s n=0003 p=Y><w NP1>LEBANON<w GE>'S <w JJ>new <w NN1>President<c YCOM>, <w NNB>Mr <w NP1>Rene <w NP1>Muawad<c YCOM>, <w RT>yesterday <w VVD>worked <w TO>to <w VVI>weld <w JJ>old <w NN>militia <w NN2>foes <w II>into <w AT1>a <w NN1>cabinet <w TO>to <w VVI>govern <w APPGE>his <w JJ>divided <w NN1>country <w CS>while <w JJ>fellow <w NN2>Christians<c YCOM>, <w VVG>demonstrating <w II>against <w PPHO1>him<c YCOM>, <w VVD>shut <w DB>half <w IO>of <w NP1>Beirut<c YSTP>. </s>

To some readers, this will be seen merely as a typical corpus text file; to others it will appear to be an unearthly and unreadable mess. As far as *MP 2.2* is concerned, this sample text is well-structured and hence can be manipulated easily for the user's convenience. For our purposes, we can divide the file contents into three different types of information: (i) tags (or normal tags) illustrated above by <text decl=...> and by <p>; (ii) part-of-speech tags, which here precede the word they categorise and which appear in a form such as <w NP1>, which is interpreted in this notation as *w* for word and *NP1* for singular Proper Name; and (iii) the words themselves (e.g., *Lebanon*).

As described below, it is possible to indicate in TAG SETTINGS the form of these different annotations and once we have done that, the program will help us manage the complexity of the corpus by, for example, suppressing the normal tags and part-of-speech tags so that, if desired, the mark-up doesn't appear at all in the display of the corpus (or in the search results). Suppressing the tags in this way will cause the excerpt from *the BNC Sampler* shown above to be displayed as follows.

suppress tags
Lebanon leader builds cabinet

By Reuter in Beirut

LEBANON'S new President, Mr Rene Muawad, yesterday worked to weld old militia foes into a cabinet to govern his divided country while fellow Christians, demonstrating against him, shut half of Beirut.

Alternatively, the normal tags and words can be suppressed so that we get a view of the corpus as though it consisted only of part-of-speech tags.

<w NP1> <w NN1> <w VVZ> <w NN1> <c YSTP>
<w II> <w NP1> <w II> <w NP1>

<w NP1> <w GE><w JJ> <w NN1> <c YCOM> <w NNB> <w NP1> <w NP1> <c YCOM> <w RT> <w VVD> <w TO> <w VVI> <w JJ> <w NN> <w NN2> <w II> <w AT1> <w NN1> <w TO> <w VVI> <w APPGE> <w JJ> <w NN1> <w CS> <w JJ> <w NN2> <c YCOM><w VVG> <w II> <w PPHO1> <c YCOM><w VVD> <w DB> <w IO> <w NP1> <c YSTP>

These suppress/display options (shown in Figure 4) provide alternative views of the texts (and search results), but whatever view is adopted, all the words and tag information in the corpus can be part of the search query. Thus all aspects of the corpus are searchable and yet there is control over the components that are displayed.

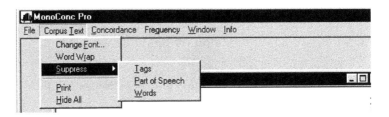

Figure 4: Suppressing tags

27

To fully exploit the information in a corpus it is often necessary to work with tags; however, it is possible to use *MP 2.2* without knowing about all the details related to tagging discussed in the remainder of this section. You may therefore want to move to the next section and come back to the tag-related information discussed below once the basics of searching and sorting have been mastered.

It is worth pointing out that while you may welcome the opportunity to work with the rich resources offered by an annotated text, such annotations typically reflect someone else's classification system. A tagged text is an analysed text. You may find that your search queries are being overly influenced by the nature of the available mark-up.

pre-processing Since there is no single, conventional way of indicating mark-up, it is necessary to tell the program about the format of the tags used in the corpus. Once this is done, the program is able to distinguish the mark-up or tags from the text itself, which ultimately makes it easier for the user to analyse the corpus. (Technical note: The results of this pre-processing procedure are stored in a temporary file on the hard disk).

cancel The COLLECT TAG INFORMATION routine starts automatically whenever a corpus file is loaded. If the corpus consists of simple text files with no mark-up or if you are only interested in performing a quick, simple search, then this stage may be bypassed. In addition, this procedure can be invoked at any time after corpus loading and may, in fact, be invoked automatically if the user selects a command such as DISTRIBUTION which relies on the information collected by this routine.

We discussed above the use of the information in TAG SETTINGS for suppressing the display of different components of the corpus files. There are other uses of this information that are discussed in the appropriate sections below, but to give an overview of the range of uses of this information, we can say that the results of the COLLECT TAG INFORMATION procedure are employed in the following procedures.

- display/suppress normal tags (mark-up)

- display/suppress part-of-speech tags

- display/suppress words

- identify location of tags in the text

- show "tracked tags"

- separate words and tags for frequency/sorting procedures

- count words
- count lines
- show distribution of hits

The meaning of all of these procedures may not be immediately apparent, but the list serves to give a sense of the extent to which the COLLECT TAG INFORMATION routine affects the operation of the program. As mentioned above, if the tag collection process is not run, the program will not display the word count for the corpus and will only give the corpus file size (in K).

2.2.4 Normal Tags

To set the form of tags, we select TAG SETTINGS from the FILE menu and choose NORMAL TAGS. The most important components that need to be identified are the TAG START and TAG STOP symbols, which are often < and >. A typical set of tag settings is shown in Figure 5 below.

Figure 5: Defining normal tags and tracked tags

Once this information is entered and COLLECT TAG INFORMATION has been run, *MP 2.2* will distinguish between mark-up and text to the extent shown in the following table.

Action	Text/Tag Distinction
Text Search	No
Regex Search	No
Tag Search	Yes
Sorting	Yes
Collocate Frequency	Yes
Corpus Frequency	Yes/No
Display/Suppress	Yes
Word Count	Yes/No

Let us briefly examine a couple of options presented in the table. The simple text search does not distinguish text and mark-up, which means that a search for **name** will find *name* occurring in the tag *<name>* and instances of *name* in the text itself. Similarly, a (case insensitive) search for **at** will find all the instances of both the word *at* and the tag *AT* assuming that they both occur in the corpus. In contrast, the TAG SEARCH, which is described in detail in Section 6, allows searches that distinguish words and/or part-of-speech tags and consequently is marked in the table as being sensitive to the text/tag distinction. A search for **AT&** will find the word *AT*, and **&AT** will find words tagged as *AT*, i.e., articles.

SKIP TAGS The corpus frequency command will either include tagnames in the count or ignore them, according to the setting of SKIP TAGS in FREQUENCY OPTIONS. If SKIP TAGS is selected, tag names are excluded from the corpus frequency count. What you think of as tag names may not always be excluded. If the tag sequence is <SP CLINTON>, then neither SP nor CLINTON will be included in the frequency count, but if the tag sequence is <SP>CLINTON</SP>, then CLINTON will be counted; only SP will be excluded.

page/para # It is possible to locate the line number and in some cases the page or paragraph number of a particular hit. To make the program track line numbers, go to NORMAL TAGS in TAG SETTINGS and select DISPLAY LINE NUMBERS . If your corpus indicates pages by means of mark-up such as <p>, then enter **<p>** in the page delimiter text box and select DISPLAY PAGE

NUMBERS. The program will simply count these tags. If there are 234 instances of <p> occurring in the corpus before a particular search item, displays the information as follows: Page 234.

There is a further box, labelled RELATIVE LINES. Select this box if you want the line numbers to be shown for a particular page such that the location of a particular hit is given as, for instance, page 6 line 2 rather the absolute line number (line 182).

tracked tags   It is clearly useful to be able to track the location of hits (by filename and page/line number), but if the structure of a corpus is encoded by the use of tags, then it will also be possible to inspect the links between individual concordance lines and particular tags. For example, in the CPSAE sub-corpus, we might want to know, for each concordance hit, who the speaker is. Since the identity of the speaker is encoded using speaker tags, all we have to do is indicate to the program that these speaker tags should be "tracked." Doing this will also allow us to sort the results on the basis of the tracked tag, as described in Section 11.3.

The TRACKED TAGS feature allows us to identify the value of the speaker tag for any of the lines in the concordance results. This means that even if the speaker tag is not visible in the concordance line, the speaker can be identified by simply clicking on the appropriate line. Selecting a line in this way causes the file name, line number and any TRACKED TAGS to appear in the lower left of the *MP* 2.2 window.

display info   If there is too much information to display in this way, an alternative is to click on a concordance line using the right mouse button. This action evokes a pop-up window and the user can then select the item DISPLAY INFO and all the tracking information for that line will be shown. (This information can optionally be included in saved and printed versions of the concordance results.)

To specify one or more TRACKED TAGS, go to TAG SETTINGS in the FILE menu and select NORMAL TAGS. Choose ADD in the TRACKED TAGS section of the resulting dialogue box, enter a name for the tag and enter the tag start and tag stop information, for example, either SP and /SP or <SP> and </SP>. (See the screen shot in Figure 5.) For a COCOA style tag, such as <A Dickens>, select internal information and enter A in TAG START, and leave TAG END empty. Note: it is necessary to re-run COLLECT TAG INFORMATION if any major changes are made in TAG SETTINGS.

2.4 Loading and unloading a corpus

Let us examine the options for loading a corpus, that is, making one or more text files available for processing by *MP 2.2*. This operation is initiated by choosing LOAD CORPUS FILE(S) from the FILE menu (Figure 6) or by issuing the CTRL-L command.

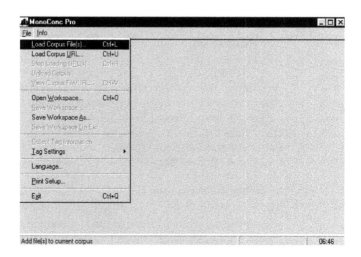

Figure 6: The FILE menu

When the LOAD CORPUS FILE(S) command is given, the typical Windows dialogue box appears in which the contents of the current directory are displayed. Alternative directories/drives can be selected via the text box at the top of the dialogue box (Figure 7).

multiple files   Further control over the display of file names is accomplished by entering a combination of characters and * in the box FILE NAME in the lower part of the dialogue box. Here it is possible to enter a string such as **g*.spo** (and press the Enter key) in order to display just those files that start with a G and have the extension SPO. Once the appropriate file name appears, use the mouse to click on the filename to select it. To select several files, use the shift and cursor keys, or CTRL-A (or to select non-adjacent files, use Ctrl and shift and click). Clicking on OPEN (or pressing Enter) loads the selected files into *MP 2.2*, making them available for searching. As discussed above, the program scans the files looking for information about tags etc. (shown in Figure 8) before the contents of the first file in the corpus are displayed in a scrollable window (Figure 9). This pre-processing of the corpus files can be cancelled at any time.

32

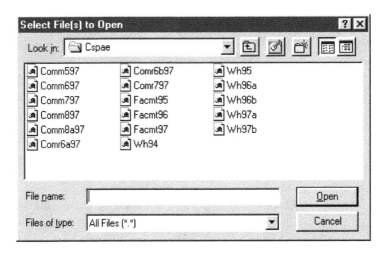

Figure 7: Selecting files making up the corpus

size limit

There is no fixed limit to the size of the corpus loaded. The corpus files appear to be loaded in the program ready for searching, but in processing the data, *MP 2.2* actually swaps chunks of text in and out of memory, with the result that the program should be able to handle any size of text. There may, however, be a limit on the number of files loaded.

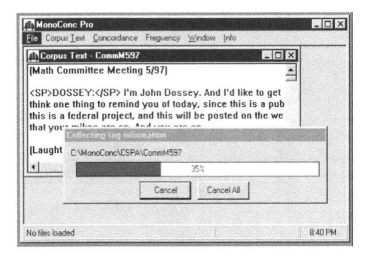

Figure 8: Collecting tag information procedure

33

2.4.1 Count words

In the FILE menu is the command COUNT WORDS WHILE LOADING. If this option is checked, then after the COLLECT TAG INFO process is complete, the number of word tokens and word types will be displayed in the lower right of the window. This slows the loading process a little and so if a word count is not needed (or you plan to create a full word frequency list), then you can leave this command unchecked.

2.4.2 Files in different directories

To load files contained in different directories, simply repeat the load file process. This repeated application of load files adds files cumulatively to the corpus and does not remove files previously installed.

Once a corpus is loaded, some new menu items related to the analysis and display of the text appear on the menu bar. These are FILE, CORPUS TEXT, CONCORDANCE, FREQUENCY, WINDOW and INFO. In addition, looking at the screen in Figure 9 we see information in the lower left corner relating to the number of the files loaded and in the lower right corner a word count for the corpus. Any of the corpus files can be examined using the scroll bars or the PageDown, End keys, etc.

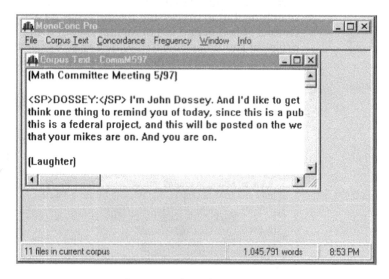

Figure 9: View of a corpus file

If several corpus files are open and the screen is too cluttered, select HIDE ALL from the CORPUS TEXT menu to close all the corpus text windows. Even if you "hide" all the corpus files, they are still available for searching and so the CONCORDANCE

34

and FREQUENCY menus remain visible. (The CORPUS TEXT menu, however, is not available when all the files are hidden.)

2.4.3 Keeping different subcorpora

One good way of organising and accessing different corpora is to maintain each subcorpus as a workspace. This option will use up a certain amount of disk space, but the advantage is that clicking on a single (appropriately named) file will load a sub-corpus, along with the settings for that sub-corpus. For more information on workspaces, see Section 7.

2.5 Load Corpus URL (Web page)

accessing web   If your computer is linked to the web, you can load one or more web documents to create a corpus. This feature allows you to use *MP 2.2* to analyse web pages. Executing the LOAD CORPUS URL command leads to the downloading of a web page to your computer to create the corpus.

Note that it is the html source which is loaded rather than the webpage as it appears in your browser and so it will be important to configure tag settings so that the mark-up, in this case html tags, can be hidden from view. In other words, it will be beneficial to make sure that the tag start and tag stop are defined as < and >, respectively.

Choosing LOAD CORPUS URL, or CTRL-U, opens a window in which the URL or web address can be entered. The form of the address should conform to the following format.

(http/ftp):/ / [user[:password]@]server[:port][/ path]

This description collapses a range of types of web address. As a start, you can load a very simple test file on the Athelstan website by entering the address: *http://www.athel.com/test.html*.

Sometimes it is best to navigate through the website to get to the appropriate location. Then, just select and copy the URL from your browser and paste it into the OPEN URL text box in *MP 2.2*. For example, the site of a speech by Tony Blair, the British Prime Minister, resides at :
http://www.number-10.gov.news.asp?NewsId=482&SectionId=32.
(Naturally, another alternative is to cut-and-paste the contents of the website to create a corpus file.)

It is possible to connect to ftp sites requiring an "anonymous" login (with the user's email address given as the password). The appropriate format for such a site is illustrated by the following example:

*ftp://anonymous:barlow@athel.com@sunsite.unc.edu/pub/docs/books
/gutenberg/etext9/bwulf10.txt*

If you wish to load the information from an ftp site that does not require an anonymous login, the form of the address would resemble the following:

ftp://ftp.hp.com/pub/networking/software/readme.txt

Since web documents must be retrieved over the net, the loading process is more complex than it is for loading text files.

When a URL is chosen, two processes are set in motion: (i) the normal COLLECT TAG INFORMATION routine, indicated by a progress bar, and (ii) the loading of the contents of the distant site, which is indicated by the reddening of a blue bar at the bottom of the window. To stop the first process, click Cancel. To stop the second process, select STOP LOADING URL(S) from the file menu (or enter CTRL-R).

2.6 Displaying the corpus files

view corpus
Once the corpus files are open, the CORPUS TEXT menu, which contains commands relating to the display and printing of the corpus file, becomes available. In many situations the corpus files will not be examined directly, but if they are to be examined, the commands CHANGE FONT and WORD WRAP control the size and positioning of the text on the screen. The SUPPRESS command leads to three choices: TAGS, PART OF SPEECH, and WORDS. Choosing one or two of the three options will lead to the non-display of the selected text objects. The suppression of the tags was illustrated above. (See also, Section 10.)

2.7 Changing the corpus

unload corpus
In addition to manipulating the form of the corpus files, it is possible to alter the actual composition of the corpus. For instance, all the files may be removed by choosing UNLOAD CORPUS from the FILE menu. This returns the program to its initial state, with only the FILE and INFO menus available. All other windows and menus are closed.

remove files
The selective removal of one or more files is accomplished by selecting VIEW CORPUS FILE from the FILE menu, selecting one or more files and clicking on the REMOVE button.

add files
To add new files to the existing corpus, simply repeat the LOAD CORPUS FILE(S) command.

2.3 Printing the corpus file

Setting up the printer is accomplished by the command PRINT SETUP in the FILE menu. (To specify the default printer, use the control panel.) If you want to print the current corpus file, the one in the active window, select PRINT from the CORPUS TEXT menu or enter CTRL-P. Since the corpus file may be large and the print command may be selected in error, a dialogue box appears, giving an estimate of the size of the file. The print job can then be cancelled if necessary.

3. Word Lists and Frequency Lists

word list

It is sometimes instructive to destroy the structure of a text in order to reveal patterns hidden by the normal linear arrangement. The most radical transformation of a text used in linguistic analyses is to rip it apart to produce a word list. Creating a word list involves snipping the text at particular places, typically the spaces between words, and counting the resulting tokens. Even though *MP* 2.2 automatically produces the word list on the execution of the relevant command, it is important to be aware of the existence of choices made in performing this transformation, as well as of the uses that can be made of the transformed text. (See Section 9.7 for a detailed discussion on the definition of words.)

Transforming a text into list of words removes the context for individual words, which means that all the linear context, i.e., all syntagmatic information, is eliminated. Consequently, it is not possible to use a word list to analyse how the information in the text is presented, but it can give an idea of what information is in the text.

The most frequent words in a text are grammatical or function words. This makes sense because each sentence contains the same grammatical words, but hopefully the content words change from one sentence to the next. Typically, the most frequent content words in a corpus are of interest since they give the best indication of the nature of the corpus and sometimes a stop list is used.

In most cases, all words occurring more than two or three times in the corpus are displayed either in frequency order (from most to least frequent) or in alphabetical order. Importantly, there are other options, however, as discussed below.

3.1 Zipf's Law and frequency bands

Below is a word frequency list for the first paragraph above in frequency order with the order or rank of the words indicated by the number in the left column.

1	12	the
2	7	of
3	5	to
4	4	a
5	4	text
6	3	in
7	3	word
8	3	list
9	3	it
10	3	is

Figure 10: Frequency list

As usual, we have function words at the top of the list with the frequency of the words trailing off rapidly as we move down the list. If you multiply the rank times the frequency of occurrence of each word, you obtain the same figure, more or less. The very top ranked words tend to be a little out, but nevertheless there is a clearly identifiable relationship holding between rank and frequency. This is called Zipf's Law, although actually there are several laws put forward by Zipf.

Examining this simple frequency list enables us to get a sense of the general form of such lists both in terms of the relation of function and content words and in the shape of the list (shown in a graph?). The severe disruption of the text needed to produce word lists means that an incredible amount of information is lost. We don't know whether *walks* is a noun or a verb or even if *the* is an article or an acronym.

To find out the distribution of words in the entire corpus, choose CORPUS FREQUENCY DATA and select either FREQUENCY ORDER or ALPHABETICAL ORDER.

3.2 Frequency options

Choosing FREQUENCY OPTIONS allows the frequency list to be tailored to fit particular requirements. It is possible to limit the data presented in three main ways, as can be seen from the FREQUENCY AND COLLOCATION OPTIONS dialogue box shown in Figure 11. First, we can set the maximum number of lines in the frequency list (using the MAXIMUM LINES parameter), which means that it is a simple matter to find, for example, the twenty most frequent words or the hundred most frequent words in a corpus. Secondly, a lower frequency boundary can be selected (MINIMUM FREQUENCY). In Figure 11, the minimum frequency has been set to 3, which means that words occurring only once or twice, of which there are many, will be excluded from the list.

The third main option is to set an upper frequency boundary (MAXIMUM FREQUENCY) that excludes words occurring more often than the set threshold. (The setting of 0, shown above in Figure 11, is used to indicate no upper boundary.)

With these parameters, it is possible to examine various frequency lists for a corpus. The most common uses are to list the most frequent words or, alternatively, to display those words that occur just once.

The two checkboxes in the dialogue box (IGNORE CASE OF LETTERS and SKIP TAGS) control case-sensitivity and tag-sensitivity in frequency calculations.

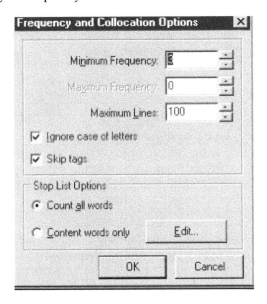

Figure 11: Frequency and collocation options

The program provides other information that can be used in various frequency-based calculations. Before the COLLECT TAG INFORMATION routine has been run, the size (in K) of the corpus is displayed. Once the COLLECT TAG INFORMATION has done its work, the size of files making up the corpus is replaced by a total word count.

41

The frequency of the keyword is given by the total number of hits—assuming, of course, that the whole corpus was searched and the search did not end prematurely. In any case, even with an incomplete search it may still be possible to estimate the total frequency of the search word in the corpus by observing the percentage of the corpus that was scanned before the search ended.

3.3 Stop list

Because grammatical or function words such as *the* are both of high frequency and generally not very interesting, it is often desirable to omit them and concentrate on words of interest which might otherwise be masked by the more frequent forms.

exclude words   There are two ways to exclude a set of words from consideration. One option is to create and load a text-only file containing the words to be excluded from the frequency listings—a stop list. The second is to add words to the stop list from within the program. Both these functions are accessed via FREQUENCY OPTIONS. To exclude a particular set of words from the frequency counts, select CONTENT WORDS ONLY, then choose EDIT, and type in the words to be omitted, Alternatively, you can load a file containing the words you wish to exclude from the frequency counts. (The words should be listed one to a line in the file.)

3.4 Batch frequency

save to file   It is possible to direct the corpus frequency results to be saved directly in a file by choosing BATCH FREQUENCY DATA from the FREQUENCY menu. The results can be saved in frequency order or alphabetical order.

3.5 Corpus comparison

Creating and saving a frequency list to file for a reference corpus allows the possibility of comparison with other corpora. Once the frequency list for the reference corpus has been saved to a file, create a frequency list for the current corpus. The CORPUS COMPARISON command then becomes available and allows the user to select the file containing the reference frequency list. (The frequency window must be active otherwise the CORPUS COMPARISON command will be greyed out.)

The program then compares the two frequency lists and produces a corpus comparison table, as shown in Figure 12.

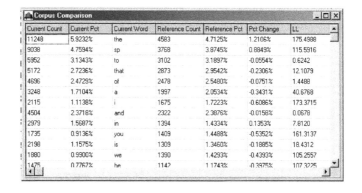

Current Count	Current Pct	Current Word	Reference Count	Reference Pct	Pct Change	LL
11248	5.9232%	the	4583	4.7125%	1.2106%	175.4988
9038	4.7594%	sp	3768	3.8745%	0.8849%	115.5916
5952	3.1343%	to	3102	3.1897%	-0.0554%	0.6242
5172	2.7236%	that	2873	2.9542%	-0.2306%	12.1079
4696	2.4729%	of	2478	2.5480%	-0.0751%	1.4488
3248	1.7104%	a	1997	2.0534%	-0.3431%	40.6768
2115	1.1138%	i	1675	1.7223%	-0.6086%	173.3715
4504	2.3718%	and	2322	2.3876%	-0.0158%	0.0678
2979	1.5687%	in	1394	1.4334%	0.1353%	7.8120
1735	0.9136%	you	1409	1.4488%	-0.5352%	161.3137
2198	1.1575%	is	1309	1.3460%	-0.1885%	18.4312
1880	0.9900%	we	1390	1.4293%	-0.4393%	105.2557
1475	0.7767%	he	1142	1.1743%	-0.3975%	107.3225

Figure 12: Corpus comparison results

The columns in the table are Current Count, Current Percentage, Current Word, Reference Count, Reference Percentage, Percentage Change, Log Likelihood[1].

The table can be sorted according to one or more of these parameters. For example, to see the words occurring in the reference corpus, but not the current corpus, we can rearrange the table to show the words occurring 0 times. Choose SORT from the FREQUENCY menu with the settings shown below.

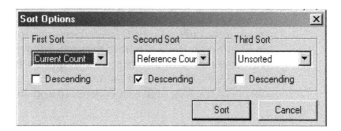

Figure 13: Sorting the comparison results

The second sort in this dialogue box will order the words in the reference corpus that were not present in the current corpus with the most frequent words at the top. The transformed table is shown in Figure 14.

---

[1] See P. Rayson and R. Garside. 2000. Comparing corpora using frequency profiling. In Proceedings of the workshop on Comparing Corpora. ACL 2000. Hong Kong.

43

Current Count	Current Pct	Current Word	Reference Count	Reference Pct	Pct Change	LL
0	0.0000%	dossey	497	0.5110%	-0.5110%	-1.0000
0	0.0000%	naep	244	0.2509%	-0.2509%	-1.0000
0	0.0000%	phillips	225	0.2314%	-0.2314%	-1.0000
0	0.0000%	burrill	167	0.1717%	-0.1717%	-1.0000
0	0.0000%	kifer	157	0.1614%	-0.1614%	-1.0000
0	0.0000%	seeley	145	0.1491%	-0.1491%	-1.0000
0	0.0000%	mandel	112	0.1152%	-0.1152%	-1.0000
0	0.0000%	silver	91	0.0936%	-0.0936%	-1.0000
0	0.0000%	bass	90	0.0925%	-0.0925%	-1.0000
0	0.0000%	constructed	81	0.0833%	-0.0833%	-1.0000
0	0.0000%	open-ended	74	0.0761%	-0.0761%	-1.0000
0	0.0000%	calculators	64	0.0658%	-0.0658%	-1.0000
0	0.0000%	alnebra	60	0.0617%	-0.0617%	-1.0000

Figure 14: Sorted corpus comparison table

Let us look at another example using the MICASE corpus. Most of the files in this spoken corpus are marked for subject matter—actually the school in which the lectures, seminars, etc. occurred—which means that we find out what words are associated with academic discourse in the Biological/Health Sciences or Humanities and Arts, for example. To do this, we take the whole MICASE corpus as a reference corpus and then examine the distribution of words in the Biological Sciences sub-corpus compared with the whole corpus. The results can then be ordered in terms of the words which are most different in the subcorpus (using log likelihood in descending order). To reduce the complexity of the data, we can save just four parameters: current word, frequency, percentage change, and log likelihood. If we separate those words which are most overrepresented in the corpus from those which are most underrepresented, we get some interesting results, as the sample in the two tables in Figures 15 and 16 shows.

frequency in subcorpus	word	% change (+)	log likelihood
516	cells	0.1198%	590.5791
541	species	0.1230%	577.1094
371	cell	0.0857%	417.9707
272	d-n-a	0.0635%	317.2777
241	gene	0.0563%	281.7837
221	protein	0.0515%	256.2135
217	r-n-a	0.0507%	254.5357
290	population	0.0606%	236.7313
180	plants	0.0412%	196.3079

Figure 15: Words overrepresented in the Biology Sub-Corpus

44

frequency in subcorpus	word	% change	(-) log likelihood
4931	i	-0.5791%	535.0468
16	women	-0.0520%	247.2912
373	mhm	-0.1183%	224.8593
1571	know	-0.2103%	215.8238
164	she	-0.0840%	210.9846
480	mean	-0.1226%	202.5319

Figure 16: Words under-represented in the Biology Sub-Corpus

4. Searching for Words and Phrases

A concordancer is, at its heart, basically a search program that looks for patterns in the text based on a search query. Simple as this sounds, it can lead to sophisticated analyses of lexical, grammatical and textual structure. The advantages of using a concordance program are that it makes it possible to (i) find rare instances of words or strings; (ii) find strings in the context of other strings, e.g., the instances of *economy* occurring after <title> and before </title>; and (iii) look for particular patterns and then rearrange and concentrate similar instances so that their properties can be revealed.

3.1 Searching for patterns

Let's look at an illustration of what we mean by patterns in the text. (For a comprehensive description of language patterns, see *Pattern Grammar* by Susan Hunston and Gill Francis.) Here we can take a mundane but illustrative example and examine the question of what kinds of words typically follow the verb *speak*. Based on our intuitions about English, we might suggest prepositions such as *to* and perhaps *with,* as typically associated with *speak.* To find out what actually occurs, we need to look in a corpus for the pattern [SPEAK + word]. (For the present, we will assume that we are working with an untagged text.)

This formulation is a little misleading, as it is not possible to specify a single term SPEAK which covers the lemma or "word family" *speak.* There are ways of specifying a lemma, but for now let us assume that we have to search for actual words: *speak, speaks, speaking, spoke,* etc.

Figure 17: Concordance menu

simple search We will start off with an elementary approach, which is simply to search for all the instances of one verb form, say the base form *speak*. To do this, we select SEARCH from the CONCORDANCE menu, or enter CTRL-S, (shown in Figure 17). In the text box at the top of the dialogue box that appears (Figure 18) type in the search term **speak** and click on OK (or press Enter). The example search queries that can be found below the search box serve to remind us about the format of simple text searches—and the use of wildcards.

Note: The parameters of the search are determined by the settings in force in GENERAL SEARCH CONTROL in the ADVANCED SEARCH dialogue box and in SEARCH OPTIONS as illustrated in Figure 19. These latter settings cover such things as whether the hyphen is treated a word boundary.

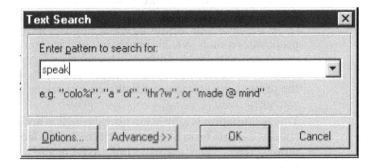

Figure 18: Performing a simple text search

If a search does not behave in the way that you expect, then this is probably because (a) the corpus is not quite what you thought it was; (b) the search term was mistyped; or (c) some setting (such as the word delimiter list) is not what you imagined.

Let us now look in some detail at what happens during the search process. In our example, the program works through the text looking for the word *speak*. With such a common word, the results should flood in fairly rapidly.

Two progress bars, shown in Figure 20, track the progression of the search as it works its way through individual files and through the corpus as a whole.

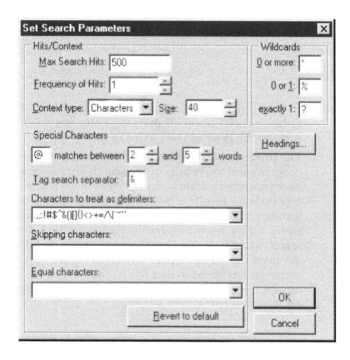

Figure 19: Settings in Search Options

search details When examining the results as they are displayed, you might wonder whether the search is case-sensitive, for example. In order to check the settings in force for a search in progress, clicking on the Details button shown in the lower right of Figure 20 will reveal the options currently selected.

49

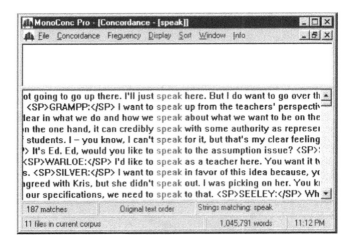

Figure 20: Progress of a search

stop a search To stop a search, but retain the hits already found, simply press
Enter or click Cancel. (If pressing Enter has no effect, simply
click on the progress box to make it active.)

The progress bars remain visible as long as the search is still in
progress and the results of the search appear in a
backgrounded window, which we will refer to as the
concordance results window (Figure 21). In this window, each
instance of the search word that the program finds is copied
along with a preceding and following context. Typically, the
search word is centred and highlighted so that the instances of
the search word line up, as shown in Figure 16. This format is
commonly referred to as a KWIC (Key Word In Context)
format. Different options for the display of concordance lines
are described in Section 10.

Figure 21: Concordance results in a KWIC format

50

preview

While the search for *speak* is in progress, it is possible to look at each line in the concordance window to see which words and prepositions frequently follow *speak*. If you want to examine the results as they are being displayed, you can simply move the progress bar window out of the way. Scrolling through the results window brings more instances into view enabling you to get a preliminary idea of the words following *speak* simply by paging through the results.

collocates

As I hope you can see on your computer, the frequent collocates of *speak* are highlighted in colour. The most frequent collocates are bright red and less frequent collocates are a duller red.

The highlighting can be turned on or off for any particular set of concordance results using the HIGHLIGHT COLLOCATES command in the DISPLAY menu.

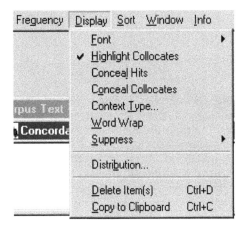

Figure 22: The Highlight Collocates command

The settings controlling the display of the collocates are in FREQUENCY OPTIONS. The appropriate span of collocates, from 1L-1R to 4L-4R can be selected along with the number of collocates to be highlighted: the top 15, for instance, for each position (1L, 1R, etc.). If function words are to be excluded, select CONTENT WORDS ONLY and enter the stop words.

51

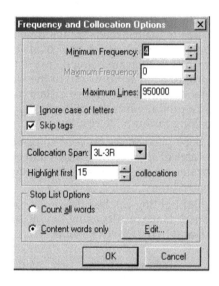

Figure 23: Settings in Frequency Options

sorting

Once the search is ended, then you can bring to bear the full power of the program to reveal patterns in the results. One way to find out which words are associated with *speak* is to sort the instances so that they are in alphabetical order of the word following the search term. The advantage of performing this 'right sort' is that all the instances of *speak to* will be next to each other in the concordance window, as will all the instances of *speak with,* and so on. The easiest way to achieve this ordering is to select 1ST RIGHT, 1ST LEFT from the SORT menu (Figure 24).

Figure 24: The Sort menu

The program then immediately rearranges the concordance lines to give a more revealing view of the search results, as shown in the sample in Figure 25.

1st R 1st L sort

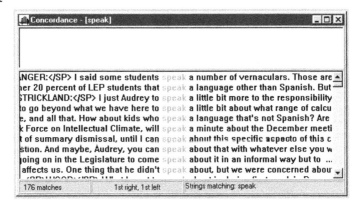

Figure 25: Sorted concordance results

You can quickly look at the words that directly follow *speak* to check that the intended re-ordering has taken place. Alternatively, you can check the description of the current sort that appears at the bottom of the results window to the right of the information on the number of hits. Having ordered the concordance lines in this way, it is very easy to see which words occur with *speak* and with what frequency. Those lines having the same word following *speak* will be clustered together, arranged according to the alphabetical order of the word *preceding* the search term (since we chose the 1ST RIGHT, 1ST LEFT sorting option). In *MP 2.2*, specifying a sorting order typically involves selecting a primary sort position (e.g., 1st Right) and a secondary sort position (e.g., 1st Left). See Section 11 for a detailed explanation of sorting.

If you scroll fairly quickly through the concordance results, you will discover that the visual patterning created by several identical words surrounding the search word will be striking enough to catch your eye. It is not necessary to focus on the results line by line; you can scan the output quite rapidly.

As described in Section 12, the program can calculate the collocates of the search term and so we could easily find the information about the frequency of prepositions associated with *speak* without actually counting individual instances.

4.2 Context window

We have seen that the results of a search are displayed in KWIC format in the concordance results window. Above this concordance window is the context window. To see a larger context (i.e., a chunk of preceding and following text) for any concordance line, simply select the line in the results window by clicking on it. This larger context is then displayed in the upper context window as illustrated in Figure 26.

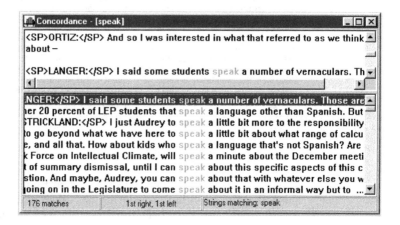

Figure 26: Context window

The context window displays the text in such a way that the highlighted keyword is visible (although the blue highlighting does not show up in these screen shots). Use the horizontal and vertical scroll bar (or use the cursor keys, PageUp, PageDown, etc.) to move around in the context window. You can try this to get a sense of the number of lines of context that is included. (The amount of the text in the Context Window is controlled by the CONTEXT WINDOW SIZE command in the DISPLAY menu. The maximum size of the context text is 30K, which is likely to be several paragraphs of text. Typically, a smaller sized context will be sufficient.)

adjust window   In our sample search for words following *speak*, it is not necessary to examine the wider context—all we really need to see in this case is the word immediately following the search word. Thus for this investigation the context window is wasting precious screen space. Fortunately, the context window and concordance window are designed to behave as parts of a split window and the relative size of each part can be adjusted. To make the concordance window larger and reduce the space taken up by the context window, position the cursor on the line between the two parts of the window. The cursor will change into an "up-down arrow" shape, which indicates that moving the mouse up or down (with the mouse button depressed) will cause the dividing line between the two parts of the window to move. In this case we want to move the dividing line upwards to increase the size of the concordance results window. Of course, on other occasions, when the search involves looking at discourse or rhetorical structures, for example, we may well want to increase the size of the context window relative to the concordance window.

The size of the window as a whole can be changed by minimising or maximising it (using the window menu or arrow icons) or by dragging the edges to whatever size is appropriate.

We can briefly summarise the results of this simple search. By scrolling through the concordance results we find the expected *speak to* and *speak with*, but also *speak on,* and *speak* (a language), etc. This simple example reveals something of the complex relation between lexical items and grammatical information. While *speak* is not usually classified as a phrasal verb, it does occur with a number or prepositions/particles: *speak about, speak against, speak on, speak up*, etc. In addition, it occurs with particular object phrases, forming mini-constructions, as in *speak the truth* and *speak Spanish.*

4.3 Searching for parts of words

4.3.1 Using wildcards

Let us consider again our search for the pattern of [SPEAK + word]. Obviously, we would get a better result if we could search for all exemplars of the lemma SPEAK: *speak, speaks, speaking, spoke,* etc. To approximate a lemma, we have to make use of wildcard characters in this simple search. (We will discuss more precise and sophisticated alternatives in Section 7.2.)

* wildcard

The first wildcard character is the asterisk *. This wildcard in a search string will match zero or more characters and therefore we can use it to formulate a more complex search string with a wider range of potential matches than would be possible using a fully specified search string. There are a couple of possibilities for defining a search string for forms of *speak* using * but the most straightforward is the search query **sp*k***, which will find all words starting with *sp* and having a *k* in them somewhere. Notice that this search string will in fact find words like *spank* and *sprocket,* as well as words that we are looking for such as *spoken.* But searches are quick and easy, and we can try out different possibilities with little cost.

We can initiate a search from the concordance menu and enter the search string **sp*k***. We could alter the string **speak**, which is in the text box from the previous search, or we can simply type in the whole search string anew. At the right end of the text box in the search dialogue box is a drop-down arrow. (See Figure 13.) Clicking on this arrow reveals a list of previous search strings. If required, one of these search queries can then be reselected to be used in a new search. In this example, there is, of course, only one previous search, but the program will store up to 20 previous searches in this list.

delete bad hits Searching for the **sp*k*** string produces numerous hits. Since we are not sure whether we have any other words apart from SPEAK, we can sort the concordance lines with respect to the search word. This means that the lines are sorted according to the alphabetical order of all the words that fit the template **sp*k***. To accomplish this, choose SEARCH TERM, 1ST RIGHT from the SORT menu. Once we have done this, we can scroll through the concordance window, checking the search word. We may notice that a word such as *sparked* occurs. Since we are not interested in such words, we select the concordance line (or lines) that contains *sparked* and press CTRL-D to delete that particular line (or select DELETE ITEM from the DISPLAY menu). When all the remaining key words are part of the desired lemma SPEAK, we can sort 1ST RIGHT, SEARCH TERM to get the information we need on the prepositions and other words following SPEAK. (You might consider the consequences of switching the sort order from SEARCH TERM, 1ST RIGHT to 1ST RIGHT, SEARCH TERM.)

? wildcard The wildcard character ? stands for a single alphanumeric character. If we search for *speak* and then want to follow up with another search which finds the other members of the SPEAK lemma (*speaks, speaking, spoke, spoken*), but not *speak* itself, then we need to use ? to ensure the presence of at least one character following the *k* in *speak*.

% wildcard The special character % represents zero or one character. Using ? and % for members of the SPEAK lemma apart from the bare form *speak*, we can enter the search term **sp?%k?%%**. The combination of **?%** following **sp** matches at least one and at most two characters, so it will find forms based on the stem *speak*, which has two vowels between *sp* and *k*, and forms based on the string *spoke*, which has only one vowel separating the stem consonants. (I will leave it as an exercise for the reader to work out what the **?%%** following **k** will match and why the word *speak* will not be found by this search, but *spoken* will.)

* alone It is a feature of *MP 2.2* that it does not require there to be an alphanumeric character within the search string. You might like to think about the results of a search for * by itself—or you could try it.

Other, more useful searches not involving alphabetic characters can be specified. For instance, it is possible to search for five-letter words (or five-digit numbers), for instance, by specifying **?????**. Alternatively, words five characters or more can be selected by specifying the search string **?????***. And sometimes it is desirable to exclude shorter words by adding a sequence of ?s. For example, to search for participial forms in English it may be preferable to search for the string **???*en** rather than ***en**, since the latter would capture a number of unwanted words such as *Ben* and *then*.(Doing this will unfortunately also exclude the short participial forms such as *seen* and *been*.)

If you want to search for question mark (?) as a literal character, you will have to substitute a different symbol for the wildcard in the SEARCH OPTIONS dialogue box. (See Section 9.8.)

Below is a summary of the wildcard characters relevant for a TEXT SEARCH:

*   matches zero or more alphanumeric characters

%   matches zero or one character

?   matches exactly one character

search and tag As the final issue relating to simple text searches, let us return to the distinction between text and tags. Clearly, it is desirable to distinguish between the content of the tags (e.g., SP) and what is being said, but in the selection from the corpus below, we can see that we have three types of text object: tags enclosed by angle brackets (<SP>), the speaker's name (Clinton) and the words actually spoken.

<SP>CLINTON:</SP> I thought I should come in and get you out of hot water, since that's what you've been doing for me for years.

The complication in the above example is that the speaker's name (**Clinton**) is conceptually a part of the tag (not part of what is spoken). This may not be a problem, but if we want to distinguish **Clinton** as speaker from *Clinton* as a spoken word, there are a couple of options we can explore. One way to restrict a search so that it only locates the spoken instances of *Clinton* is to remove < and > from the list of word delimiters. (See Section 9.7.) You may need to think about this for a minute—and if you do ponder this situation, you will realise that, in fact, only > needs to be removed from the word delimiter list.

Another option that may be open to you is to adopt a different style of tags. For instance, in the COCOA tag format, **Clinton** as speaker is internal to the tag, as in <SP Clinton>. This style of annotation makes a clear conceptual distinction between speaker tag and spoken text, although the text inside the tag is not opaque to searches.

4.4 Saving the concordance lines

To save the contents of the concordance window, select SAVE AS FILE from the CONCORDANCE menu. A dialogue box appears and the name of the results file can be entered.

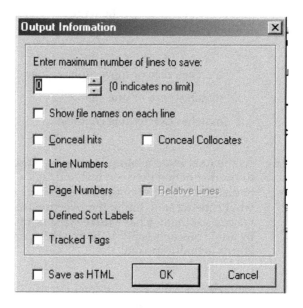

Figure 27: Saving a concordance

html   The default option is to save just the concordance results in the file. However, there are a variety of options concerning other information that can be saved along with the concordance lines, including SHOW FILE NAMES ON EACH LINE, CONCEAL HITS, LINE NUMBERS, PAGE NUMBERS, DEFINED SORT LABELS ,TRACKED TAGS, and CONCEAL COLLOCATES. The results may also be saved as an html file, which can then be displayed via the web. One advantage of doing this is that the colour information of the highlighted collocates is retained.

58

The default option is to save just the concordance results in the file. However, there are a variety of options concerning other information that can be saved along with the concordance lines. Checking the box SHOW FILE NAMES ON EACH LINE causes a preceding filename to be saved with each concordance line. The filename indicates the file in the corpus that the concordance line is associated with. Other options are CONCEAL HITS, LINE NUMBER, PAGE NUMBER, and TRACKED TAGS. (If PAGE NUMBER is selected, then RELATIVE LINES may be selected if you want to see the line number of the hit relative to the page rather than the line number in the file as a whole.) To save the concordance lines, enter a suitably descriptive file name and press the enter key (or click on OK).

For further manipulation of the text, you may need to load the results file into a word processing program such as *Word*.

If only a few examples are needed, it may be more convenient to use CTRL-C to copy the required text directly from within *MP 2.2* to the clipboard and then paste it into your document. The copy command is also available in the DISPLAY menu.

4.5 Printing the concordance results

The concordance lines can be printed by entering CTRL-P or selecting PRINT from the CONCORDANCE menu. The appropriate concordance window must be active for printing to occur.

5. The Power of Regular Expressions

The simple searches described in Chapter 4 will suffice for many purposes and are especially useful for exploratory searches. The basic TEXT SEARCH is also very useful when used in conjunction with a sort-and-delete strategy. Particular sort configurations can be chosen to cluster unwanted examples (words preceded by *a* and *the* perhaps), which can then be selected and deleted. For more complex searches, however, we need to use the ADVANCED SEARCH command. This command brings up a more intricate dialogue box (displayed in Figure 20), which at the top contains the familiar text box in which the search query is entered.

three searches The most important part of the ADVANCED SEARCH dialogue box is labelled SEARCH SYNTAX, as seen in Figure 20 below. The three radio buttons allow users to specify the kind of search they wish to perform. The first, TEXT SEARCH, refers to the basic searches described in the previous section. The REGULAR EXPRESSION search allows for search queries containing boolean operators (AND, OR and NOT). For example, a regular expression to capture the *speak* lemma might be given as **sp[eo]a?k**. This expression will match the string *sp* followed by *e* or *o*, an optional *a* and finally *k*. As we will see in the next section, this is still not precise enough to yield unwanted matches, but it is more accurate than the search query based on wildcard characters described above. (Attentive readers will already have noticed that the special character ? differs in meaning in the REGULAR EXPRESSION search and the basic TEXT SEARCH.) The third option in the advanced search dialogue box is TAG SEARCH, which allows the user to specify a search query consisting of a combination of words and tags, with the special symbol & being used to separate words from tags in the search query. For instance, the search string **that&DD** finds examples of *that* tagged as a demonstrative pronoun and **&JJ of&** finds all instances of adjectives followed by the word *of*. These three types of search will be described in detail in the following sections.

61

5.1 Text search

simple search The TEXT SEARCH option in ADVANCED SEARCH is the same as the simple SEARCH described in the previous chapter. One advantage of launching a simple search query from the ADVANCED SEARCH dialogue box is the fact that other options such as APPEND SEARCH, IGNORE CASE OF LETTERS and BATCH SEARCH are accessible.

Figure 28: Performing an advanced search

5.2 Regular Expression Search

You will be able to perform reasonable searches using the simple search option, but if you are working with non-tagged texts, you should, over time, explore the use of regular expressions since they provide a level of control that will allow you to formulate complex, precise searches.

The full complexity of regular expressions, a well-defined set of string operators, can be overwhelming at first, but it is certainly possible to make immediate use of the simpler aspects of regular expressions and to build up complex searches step-by-step. It is useful to refer to previous regular expression searches saved in the search history list, and if you create a particularly useful regular expression, you might want to use the load/save feature of BATCH SEARCH to store the search query in a file so that search strings can be retrieved rather than recreated.

AND, OR, NOT To initiate a regular expression (regex) search, select the radio button labelled REGULAR EXPRESSION located on the left side of the ADVANCED SEARCH dialogue box. See Figure 29. Note that three examples of regular expression searches appear under the search text box, as an aid to remembering the appropriate form of regex search queries.

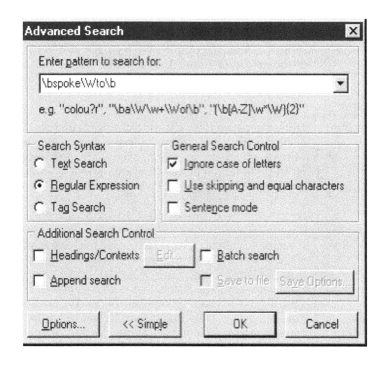

Figure 29: A search using a regular expression

string search Regex searches are string searches, which means that the computer searches for the string anywhere in the text, regardless of word boundaries or other surrounding text. Thus, if *let* is specified as the search term, then *letter, toilet* and *complete* are all potential matches for this search term.

\<word\> Because regex searches are string searches, word boundaries must be indicated explicitly and there are a variety of ways to do this. The basic method is to use symbols for the left and right boundaries, \< and \>, as in \<let\>. Or, if you wish to find words starting with the letter z, you could search for \<z. If you try this, you will see that only the initial z of the word is

63

highlighted and to order the z words in alphabetical order you must choose a 1st right sort. You then see among the common z-words like *zero* and *zone* some other interesting specimens, which are either creative productions like *zodiacally, zombified,* and *zeppelin-buttocked,* which I can understand (more or less), to borrowings which are new to me, such as *zagara, zaibatsu,* and *zazen.*

Similarly, if you wish to find words ending in *z*, you can search for **z\>**.

\bword\b   A more general and slightly easier way of specifying a word boundary is by using the meta-character **\b**. Thus a search for *let* can be specified as **\blet\b**. Meta-characters such as **\b** typically come in complementary pairs and in this case the alternative symbol is **\B**, which stands for a non-word boundary. Thus a search for **\Bz\B** will find all those words which contain *z* surrounded by non-word boundaries—that is, by other letters or numbers.

delimiter\W   How can a search for the phrase *spoke to* be specified? One way to capture this is by means of the search string **\bspoke\b \bto\b**, which includes the space character between the two word boundary symbols. One alternative to entering the space character is to use the whitespace meta-character **\s**, which covers both space and tab. However, whitespace does not cover all word delimiters and therefore in order to avoid missing some instances of the phrase *spoke to* it is better to use the meta-character **\W**, which stands for any symbol that is a word delimiter; in other words, it covers all the characters listed as word delimiters in SEARCH OPTIONS, along with space, Enter, etc. Thus the alternative search string for *spoke to* is **\bspoke\Wto\b** (or **\Wspoke\W\to\W**), which is based on non-word characters rather than the word boundary. (It is not necessary to specify word boundaries and search for **\bspoke\b\W\bto\b**; the simpler query above yields the same results.)

You might think about how likely it is that **spoke\Wto** will give the same results. (Certainly, this search string will find all instances of *spoke to*, but it may also snare other strings if the corpus contains phrases such as *spoke together*.)

A solid session reading about regular expressions is not much fun, and here, in particular, time reading this text should be interspersed with generous periods of experimentation. In general, it is best to try out different regex searches, starting with simple searches and increasing the complexity of the expression symbol by symbol. It is also true that regexes created one day look opaque, even to their creator, the next day. Useful regexes should be saved in a file with a descriptive label.

While there is a generally agreed core of regex forms, each software program that includes them has its own idiosyncrasies due to the general context within which the regular expressions operate. Even if you are familiar with regex syntax, you will need to experiment with a variety of options to see how regular expression searches are implemented in *MP* 2.2.

[aeiou]   Square brackets are used to indicate choices, as in [eo], which matches one character, *e* or *o*. In addition, it is possible to specify a choice of a set of characters, as in **[0123456789]**, which can be also be given as the range **[0-9]**. Letters and numbers can be specified as **[0-9a-zA-Z]**, but remember that despite the length of this range only one alphanumeric character encountered in the text is matched by this search term; square brackets are always associated with just a single character in the text.

\d \w \D \W   Metacharacters are commonly used in place of the standard ranges. Thus \d is any digit, equivalent to [0-9]. The metacharacter \w is equivalent to any alphanumeric character, but in addition to digits and numbers, it includes characters not listed as word delimiters in SEARCH OPTIONS. Conversely, \D is any non-digit and, as discussed above, \W is any non-alphanumeric.

OR | Let us return to the question of how regular expressions can be used in a lemma search. One possibility is to use | to indicate logical "or" as in \bspeak\b | \bspeaks\b | \bspoke\b | \bspoken\b etc. In general, parentheses are used to indicate the scope of a disjunction. In this case, however, they are not necessary since strings take precedence over disjunction. (In other words, the first part of the search query specified above is not interpreted as a search for **speak** followed by \b or \b.)

a? = optional a   Another way to perform this lemma search is to specify the query **speaks?** | **spoken?** which includes two kinds of disjunction, | and ?. The question mark is a rather specialised form of disjunction and is typically classified as a counter, which means zero or one instance of the symbol specified. The search string **s?** or **[s]?** stands for *s* or zero (nothing). Other similar forms of counters are s+ and s*, which are equivalent to one or more *s* and zero or more *s*. (Note the difference in the use of * in a simple text search where it is equivalent to zero or more characters and here where it means zero or more instances of the preceding expression—*s* in this case.)

greed   In some situations, searches involving the use of + and * will match a larger than expected chunk of text. This is because these operators match the maximum string possible: a feature known as greediness.

An alternative search string we could enter is **sp[eo]a?k[se]?n?**, which finds words containing *sp* followed by *e* or *o*, and an optional *a*, followed by *k*, an optional *s* or *e*, and finally, an optional *n*. Since we did not specify a word boundary, the search will also capture *outspokenly* and perhaps exotica (in English texts) such as words like *prospekt*.

lemma The search string **\bsp[eo]a?k[sei]?n?g?\b** does a good job at capturing the SPEAK lemma, including *speaking*. Since these strings are fairly complex you should definitely take advantage of the fact that, as mentioned above, the previous search strings are available from the drop-down box at the end of the search text box. A separate search term history is maintained for each of the three types of advanced search.

scope If we wish to search for *speak* followed by either *to* or *with*, and we try the string **speak\Wto\b | \bwith\b**, we will find that we have specified a search for either *with* or *speak to*. To search for *speak to* or *speak with*, we need to specify the scope of the disjunction and use the search term **\bspeak\W(to\b | \bwith\b).**

while ... A complex search of a large corpus may take some time. What can you do while the search is progressing? You have several options (in addition to making a cup of coffee). For instance, you can scroll through the hits as they are displayed to start looking for interesting examples. You can also click on a line to see which corpus file it comes from and to see any other information provided in tracked tags. (The information is displayed in the lower left of the window.) Clicking on a line will also allow you to view the larger context for the hit, which is displayed in the upper context window. Finally, you can click on the DETAILS button in the search progress window to check on the search settings in effect.

NOT ^ If you want to search for *York*, you might well be overwhelmed by instances of *New York*, even in a British newspaper text. One way to avoid these instances is exclude the word *New*. To accomplish this, we can take advantage of the NOT symbol ^ and use the search string **[^N][^e][^w]\WYork\b** or simply, **[^w]\WYork\b**. If, to continue with our example, you also wanted to exclude instances of the *Duchess of York*, and *Archibishop of York*, then you might disallow both *f* and *w*, as in **[^fw]\WYork\b,** although this would also exclude *City of York*.

Turning to another example, perhaps we would like to find examples of *an* followed by a word that does not start with a vowel. To do this, we search for **\ban\W[^aeiouAEIOU]**. (Performing this search reveals some interesting results including, in a newspaper text, some errors that have occurred due to the process of writing and revising text. Looking at the results, we find that in some cases *an* turns up when it is separated from a vowel-initial noun by an intervening adjective, as in *an large order*. Presumably an earlier version of the text contained the phrase *an order* and the *an* was not converted to *a* when the adjective *large* was added.)

^ $ anchors The occurrence of ^ as the first item after [means NOT. In other positions outside of square brackets, it will be interpreted as the beginning of a line. The dollar sign $ is the anchor for the end of a line.

\1 same again Let us look at a rather different search query: \W(is|are)\W\1\W. The \1 option is essentially a way of repeating whatever is specified in the preceding parentheses. (If there is more than one set of parentheses, then \1, \2, can be used to reference the corresponding groupings.) In this particular example, the expression grouped by parentheses contains a disjunction and the query will match instances of *is is* and *are are*. A simple text search (or two) could replicate this search, but there are searches that would be much more difficult to carry out using a simple text search. For example, if we wish to locate three-word alliterations, that is, sequences of three words starting with the same letter, you could use the simple text query **a* a* a***, then **b* b* b***, etc. Or you could use a single regex search: \W(\w)\w*\W\1\w*\W\1\w*\W.

{n,m} Does English allow a string of *sss* or *ssss* in a word? Or are all such occurrences likely to be typos and spelling mistakes? We could simply search for **sss**, or we can use a counter—a number enclosed by curly brackets—and search for **s{3}**. If you do this, you might find quite a few typos such as *embarrasssing*, and also some acceptable expressions such as *Yesss!* and *Pssst!* Other formulations of similar search queries are **s{3,5}** to capture *sss, ssss* and *sssss*. And to look for three or more *s*, we can search for **s{3,}**.

Here is a question. If the word *Psssst!* occurs in a text and you search for **s{3,4}**, will the word show up once, twice or three times in the hits? You might think that the hits would be *Psssst! Psssst!* and *Psssst!*. In fact, that there will only be one hit, equivalent to *Psssst!*. This is another example of greediness in action; the search term will only match the maximum string.

perfect search If we wish to search for the English perfect in an untagged corpus, then we know that we have to search for something like *has* or *have* followed by an *-en/-ed* form. This can be accomplished by the following regex search query: \bha[vs]e?\W\w{4,}e[nd]\b. The part of the search query that we hope will match the participle is "padded" with alphanumeric characters (\w) to eliminate shorter words ending in *-en* or *–ed* such as *ten* and *bed*. However, some good hits such as *seen* will also be omitted by this search query and in cases like this it is up to the user to formulate the search query in such a way as to get the right balance between a good retrieval rate and a high percentage of desired forms in the concordance results. The specification of a minimum of four letters in the participle in the search query above has the effect of increasing the percentage of good "hits" in the results, at the cost of missing some instances of the present perfect that occur in the corpus.

Let us continue with this example and make a modification to the search query to capture cases in which a word intervenes between the auxiliary and participle. Thus, to capture those strings in which an adverb (or *not* or *been*) occurs before the participle, we can add a specification for a word (at least three characters long) \W\w\w\w+\W or \W\w{3,}\W. The revised search query then becomes \bha[vs]e?\W\w{3,}\W\w{4.}e[nd]\b. And, finally, to make the adverb optional we group the "word" characters comprising the intervening word and add a counter:
\bha[vs]e?(\W\w{3,}){0,1}\W\w{4,}e[nd]\b.

You might try out a broader search query based on the following: \bha[vs]e?(\W\w+){0,2}\W\w+e[nd]\b. How do the results compare with those produced by the previous search query?

If you have followed these examples, you will have a sense of the use and power of regular expression searches. I would encourage you to experiment in building up different regex search queries. The language is very powerful and repays some attention to the details of the query syntax. You will need some time to work out the interaction between regexes and other parts of the program. For example, if you are making use of upper case in regex searches, you should make sure that IGNORE CASE OF LETTERS is not checked in the search dialogue box.

For those unsatisfied with the extent of the coverage here, there are several books devoted solely to the elucidation of regular expressions.

The table below summarises regular expression syntax.

.	any character
[a-z]	any lower case letter
[0-9]	any number
[aeuio]	any vowel (in English)
[^lr]	not l or r
\b[a-z]+\b	lower case word

68

\b[A-Z][a-z]*\b	word with upper case initial letter
\b[0-9]+\b	number
\b	word boundary
\B	word non-boundary
\d	any digit
\D	any non-digit
\w	any word character (= alphanumeric)
\W	any non-word character (defined by word delimiters)
\s	whitespace
\S	non-whitespace
*	zero or more
+	one or more
{n}	n instances of previous expression
{n,m}	from n to m instances
{n,}	at least n instances

6. The Search for Syntax

Many linguists working on syntax are considering how corpus resources can be used to provide data for linguistic analyses. A discussion of the role of corpora in syntactic analyses is well beyond the scope of this book, but we can follow (Elena Sinclair) and distinguish two ways to approach corpus data: corpus-based and corpus-driven analyses. Corpus-based and corpus-driven analyses differ in the importance for the analysis of the empirical data in a corpus. The underpinnings of a corpus-based approach might come from a theory or conjecture and the corpus is seen as a source of crucial examples which will support or reject a theoretical position. The assumption in a corpus-driven approach is that the analyses has to account for or reflect the data found in a corpus.

Words are rarer than people generally imagine to the extent that syntax involves strings of words, we are looking for instances that are even rarer. On the other hand, since syntax, in some sense, can be seen as abstracting away from particular words, we might expect some syntactic structures to be quite common, but since in practical terms most analysts will be looking for particular structures in particular configurations, then the problem is more likely to be too little data, rather than too much. For some aspects of syntax, such as the link between particular lexical items and syntactic constructions, a corpus is crucial.

6.1 Using plain texts

Finding syntactic patterns in untagged text necessarily means searching for words and making use of punctuation wherever possible. In previous chapters, we saw ways of searching for the present perfect using either a simple text search and wild card characters or the more powerful regex search commands.

Unfortunately, there is no magic way to extract syntactic patterns. We can only follow the mundane formulations of search strings that come to mind. And it has to be said that there is a certain amount of trial and error in formulating a search string that gets the best results, and, as always, there will be a tension between precision and recall. Selecting the

SENTENCE MODE checkbox in ADVANCED SEARCH may improve precision since this will not allow search string to cross a sentence boundary, which may otherwise happen if the search involves several words. Of course, if you use sentence mode, then you cannot use a search string such as *. **There** to find sentence-initial *there*. In this case perhaps a case-sensitive search for **There** will yield better results in this case since it would also find sentence-initial *there* following a sentence ending in a question mark, etc.

6.2 Using Part of Speech tags

speech_NNS

Unlike the spoken corpus described above, which in the version used here has no POS tags, the *BNC Sampler* corpus is fully tagged. To take advantage of this specialised annotation, it is necessary to indicate the distinction between part-of-speech tags and other tags. Once this is accomplished, the suppress/display options will work and, more importantly, we can perform a word/tag search. Again we select TAG SETTINGS and this time choose PART OF SPEECH TAGS. If the POS tags take a form such as *the_AT*, we select EMBEDDED IN WORD and enter _ in the DELIMITER CHARACTER box. This might be described as "attached to word." The tag is connected directly to the word by a special symbol such as _ or ^, and the end of the tag is typically a space or other word-delimiter character.

If the tags are specified, as in the *BNC Sampler*, as *<w AT>the*, then we select OUTSIDE WORD (see Figure 30) and enter <w and <c (for punctuation) in TAG START and > in TAG END. These tags, which may or may not be attached to the word, have an explicit tag end (although it would be possible to use # meaning "space" as the tag end, but this would not cover line returns, etc.) In addition, since the tag precedes the word it classifies, we must select the BEFORE WORD box.

Figure 30: Defining POS tags and meta-tags

72

6.3 Meta-tags

In the above searches, we made use of wildcard characters to capture a range of tags in the search. For example, we used the search term **NN?** to capture the tags for both singular and plural nouns, NN1 and NN2. However, the search query **NN?** also matches the tag NNB, which is used for titles such as *Mr., Lady,* and *General.* What we need is a way to specify a tag representation that covers singular and plural nouns but not titles.

define a tagset To do this, we can create a meta-tag CNOUN, which we define in the meta-tags section. We choose TAG SETTINGS from the file menu, select PART OF SPEECH TAGS and in the META-TAGS part of the dialogue box, choose ADD. Enter the name of the new meta-tag (i.e., CNOUN) and enter all the constituent tags (i.e, NN1, NN2), separated by a comma in the TAGS box. Note: In defining the tags making up a meta-tag, it is permissible to include wildcard characters in order to capture more than one tag name. Meta-meta-tags are not allowed, however; you can only use actual tags in the definition of a meta-tag.

The use of meta-tags allows the user to build on the tagset of the corpus to define a new tagset to be used in search queries. Say, for instance, that we wish to define a tag complementizer that includes *who, whom, which* and *that*, which in the Sampler are tagged as, respectively PNQS, PNQO, DDQ, and CST. It is very easy to define a new tag COMP that covers all four original tags. Once this is done, searches can be carried out using the overarching category COMP or a specific (original) category such as PNQS.

6.4 Tag Search

A corpus in which each word is annotated with part-of-speech tags provides a richer, more structured database allowing targetted searches and opening up the possibility of performing syntactic (or colligational) analyses.

It is possible to investigate a tagged corpus using a simple TEXT SEARCH or a REGULAR EXPRESSION search and in this case the search queries simply treat both the words and their tags as searchable strings of symbols. There may well be good reasons for carrying out such a search, but here we will focus on searching tagged corpora using a TAG SEARCH.

tagged corpus Let us take as an example of a tagged corpus *the BNC Sampler*, available from British National Corpus at Oxford University. A few lines from the corpus were shown above on page 26 and if you look at that sample, you will see that the POS tags, which have the form <w TAG>, are attached and precede the words they categorise. Thus, in this corpus, the adjective *old* is rendered as <w JJ>old. (Punctuation is indicated by tags of the form <c PUNC>.)

Before initiating a TAG SEARCH, information on the format of the different tags must be entered in the Part of Speech TAG SETTINGS and the COLLECT TAG INFORMATION routine must have been run. For details, see Section ?2.2.

To perform a TAG SEARCH, select ADVANCED SEARCH from the CONCORDANCE menu. Once the ADVANCED SEARCH dialogue box appears, select the TAG SEARCH radio button in the SEARCH SYNTAX section on the left of the dialogue box, as shown in Figure 31.

old&JJ

The search query in a TAG SEARCH can contain any permutation of words, tags, or words and tags. The basic syntax of the search query is **word&tag**. Note that this is the case whatever the ordering of words and tags in the corpus itself. Thus, the fact that in the *BNC Sampler* corpus the tags precede the words is irrelevant when it comes to specifying the order of words and tags in the search query. (All details about corpus format were specified in TAG SETTINGS.)

The & is used as a special symbol to distinguish specifications of words from specifications of tags. If an alternative symbol such as $ is preferred, then simply substitute $ for & in the TAG SEARCH SEPARATOR text box in SEARCH OPTIONS. (See Figure 19.)

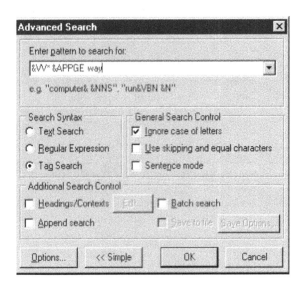

Figure 31: A Tag Search

6.5 Searching for words and tags

Having a tagged corpus opens up a lot of possibilities. We can look for different constructions, as described below, and in searching for words, we can pinpoint the forms we are interested in.

In English, in particular, there is a considerable amount of zero derivation, i.e., a lack of morphology, which means that many words have the same form whether they are verbs or nouns. Thus, while *hold* most frequently occurs as a verb, it is also a noun, as in *ship's hold*. Having a tagged corpus makes it much easier to locate the desired POS, and this becomes particularly important when we want to search for the rarer of the two forms. For instance, we can search for the noun *hold* by entering **hold&NN1** as a search term. If we want to find the plural noun form *holds*, we can use the search query **holds&NN2**. (The tags used in the tagged version of the *Corpus of Spoken Professional American English*, which some readers may be using, are almost exactly the same as those in the BNC, but, of course, other corpora may well use different tagsets and hence the particular specifications for singular and plural nouns will differ from those used in our examples here.)

wildcards ? % *   What if we want to search for both singular and plural noun forms? In this case, we can make use of the simple wildcard characters % ? * and enter the search query **hold%&NN?** or **hold%&NN***.

case sensitive   Note that if IGNORE CASE OF LETTERS is left unchecked, then the search for tags will be case sensitive.

So far I have emphasised the positive aspects of working with a tagged corpus. However, once the search is completed, a disadvantage of a tagged corpus is only too clearly evident in the cluttered appearance of the search results. Now that we have used the tags to refine our search, we will probably want to hide the POS tags, and perhaps the normal tags too, before examining the results in detail. To achieve this, select SUPPRESS in the DISPLAY menu and choose first PART OF SPEECH and then reselect SUPPRESS and select TAGS. All the mark-up will disappear and you will then be left with only the words. The idea is to have the best of both worlds: to exploit the tags in the search process and then suppress them when the results are obtained.

Whether the mark-up in the concordance results window is displayed or hidden, the collocate frequency and sorting functions will always ignore the tags and work solely on the words. (To avoid this state of affairs, it would be necessary to prevent the collection of the tag identifier information by the COLLECT TAG INFORMATION routine.)

75

As mentioned above, one advantage of a tagged corpus is the possibility of looking for examples of lexical / syntactic units such as the *way* construction, as illustrated by *muddle our way through* or *fight his way out*. To locate these constructions, we need to specify the sequence of verb, possessive pronoun and *way*, i.e., **&VV* &APPGE way&.**

The search provides 83 matches and we see common verbs such as *make, work* and *find*, along with verbs describing the manner of motion such as *thread* and *snake*, and also *wing* as in: *If you're one of our lucky 10, a Big Shot diffuser/dryer will be winging its way to you soon.*

Looking at the frequency of the word following the search term, we find the most frequent items are: *through* 16, *to* 12, *into* 5, *up* 4, *across* 4, *by* 3, *out* 3, *down* 3, *back* 3, *around* 3, *in* 2. The fact that all the common right collocates of this search term are prepositions illustrates very nicely the centrality of a path or directional component to this construction.

wildcard @

The search query given above finds three-word instances of the *way* construction based on Verb + Pronoun + *way*, but perhaps this is too restrictive. If we want to allow for the possibility of "intervening words" occurring in this construction, we can make use of the 'range' wildcard character @. We can set the range of @ in SEARCH OPTIONS to be 0 to 1, which means zero or one intervening words, and then search for **&VV* @ &APPGE @ way&.** As it turns out, we only get a few extra examples, in which, for example, *own* occurs before *way*.

* alone

Let us look at one final variant. If we wanted to find examples in which there is exactly one word intervening between the pronoun and *way*, we could use the special character * and search for **&VV* &APPGE * way&**

6.6 Searching for part-of-speech tags

To create a search query that locates complex noun-noun compounds consisting of five nouns, we can search for **&NN? &NN? &NN? &NN? &NN?.** Of the 52 examples found, some, such as *beep beep beep beep beep*, are not of enthralling interest and others are dubious examples. For instance, *mama mama ma ma ma* does not qualify as a noun compound. On the other hand, the search does bring out some good examples such as *Channel Tunnel Rail Link Bill, speed enforcement camera trial site,* and the almost mellifluous *Air Traffic Control information system.*

To take another example of a search for a syntactic form, we can look in the corpus for infinitive plus present participle constructions. To do this in the *BNC Sampler* corpus, we enter the search query **&TO &VVI &VVG**. (In this corpus the &TO tag covers not only *to*, but also *na* from *gonna* and *ta* from *gotta*.) The results of the search show a variety of verbs being used, with the most common being *start*, as in *to start talking*, with the phrase *to stop x-ing* being much rarer. The verbs *keep* and *continue* also occur, giving us a class of verbs that focus on the initiation, continuation and completion of actions. Another common verb is *go* and not surprisingly there are some fixed expressions such as *to go shopping* found in the corpus.

6.7 Searching for words

ignoring tags

It is simple to search for words in a tagged corpus. One way to do this is to enter the search words and &, as in **take& part&.** By default, however, you can, in fact, simply search for **take part**, without specifying the word-tag boundary explicitly. Thus, if you have a tagged corpus and you want to simply ignore the presence of tags, you just enter the words or phrase you wish to locate. (Note: this will only work in the TAG SEARCH option.)

6.8 Searching for punctuation

The *BNC Sampler* corpus contains tags for punctuation as well as tags for words. The punctuation tags have the form <c PUNC> and in the settings for PART OF SPEECH TAGS we entered both <w and <c as valid tag starts. Based on these punctuation tags, we could look for three-word sentences using the query **&YSTP * * * &YSTP**.

Note: Since the full stops (periods) will belong to different sentences, we need to ensure that SENTENCE MODE in the ADVANCED SEARCH dialogue box is not selected. In addition, even though we are searching for tags indicating full stops, we need to remove the full stop from the set of word delimiters specified in SEARCH OPTIONS.

7. Using Workspaces

avoid reload As is clear from the previous section, loading and processing a corpus can take some time. Since it is often the same set of corpus files which are loaded each time *MP* 2.2 is started, it makes sense to freeze the current state of the program, at will, so that the analysis of a corpus can be continued at any time. This is the idea behind a workspace. A workspace is saved as a special MonoConc Pro Workspace file (.mws), which can then be opened at any time to restore *MP* 2.2 to its previous state, with the corpus loaded ready for searching. Windows containing search results and frequency data are, however, not included in the saved workspace. (Only the search histories are saved.)

7.1 Saving a workspace

A workspace—the current corpus and settings of *MP* 2.2—can be saved at any time by selecting the command SAVE WORKSPACE or SAVE WORKSPACE AS from the FILE menu. The usual dialogue box appears and the name and location of the workspace file can be specified in the normal way. (Generally, it is only the links to the corpus that are saved, not a copy of the corpus itself.)

options Once a (memorable, descriptive) filename for the saved workspace has been entered, the user is asked to choose some different workspace options. If COLLECT TAG INFORMATION has been run and you want to save the information gathered during this process as a part of the workspace (thereby avoiding the re-running of COLLECT TAG INFORMATION), select the options shown in Figure 32. The line/page and the tracked tag info is saved as part of the workspace. (The saved workspace consists of a saved file and an associated folder of the same name.)

If the corpus consists of downloaded URLs, then selecting the third option in this dialogue box saves the actual contents of the corpus, which avoids the need to reload web documents.

Warning: Keep corpus files and workspace files separate. It is advisable to create a folder (called Workspaces) in which to hold all the workspace files (and their associated folders). This will make it easy to locate any given workspace file and avoid mixing of workspace files and corpus files. The first few lines of the workspace file look something like the following:

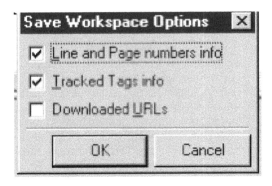

Figure 32: Options for Save Workspace

[GeneralConfiguration]
CorpusPath=C:\barlow\New Folder\
StopListPath=
ConcordancePath=C:\
[[FreqPath]]=
CorpusFreqPath=
CorpusFont=System,-12,1,-2147483640,0
SystemFont=MS Sans Serif,8,0,-2147483640,0
Language=1033
SaveOnExit=1

If you see lines like these in your loaded corpus, then you know that you have possibly loaded a workspace file as a corpus file by mistake. Once a workspace has been opened, then the user has a choice of two commands: SAVE WORKSPACE AS or simply SAVE WORKSPACE.

SAVE ON EXIT   In addition, the SAVE ON EXIT command can be selected in order to save the current workspace when the user quits the program.

80

7.2 Opening a workspace

It is possible to choose OPEN WORKSPACE from the FILE menu (or select CTRL-O) in order to load a saved workspace file. If OPEN WORKSPACE is activated when corpus files have been loaded, then those files are unloaded and replaced by the corpus specified in the workspace file.

shortcut

Hint: A quick way to open *MP 2.2* with the corpus loaded is to double-click on a saved workspace file.

tutorials

The use of workspaces should make it easier to create lab tutorials for students, since the settings and corpora needed for a series of investigations can be conveniently saved in the form of a series of workspaces: activity1, activity2, etc.

8. Performing Additional Searches

8.1 Batch search

multiple search A BATCH SEARCH has two main functions: searching for multiple items and performing a search in which the results are not displayed, but are instead written directly to a file. Let's start with the first of these.

You may be thinking that we have already covered some ways of searching for multiple items. This is true. Excluding the use of wildcard characters, we have three ways of performing a multiple-item search (e.g., a search for *apple* and *orange*): (i) a REGULAR EXPRESSION search using a disjunction (|), (ii) an APPEND SEARCH, or (iii) a BATCH SEARCH. The best way to search for *apple* and *orange* is to use a REGULAR EXPRESSION search using the query \b**apple**\b | \b**orange**\b. This method finds all the hits in one pass, unlike the other methods which require a pass through the entire corpus for each item.

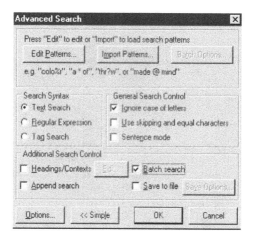

Figure 33: A Batch Search

83

Saving a query There is a third use of BATCH SEARCH and that is to re-use search patterns. While each of the search types (TEXT SEARCH, REGULAR EXPRESSION and TAG SEARCH) has a drop-down box containing a list of recent searches, only the BATCH SEARCH option allows the saving of search queries to a file.

batch search Let us step through a BATCH SEARCH, which is rather different (superficially at least) from the other kinds of searches described above. Selecting the BATCH SEARCH option causes the usual search text box to be replaced by three buttons, shown at the top of Figure 33.

The first step in specifying a search query is to click on EDIT PATTERNS. As can be seen in Figure 34, this action brings up a large search box in which multiple items can be entered. (In the example shown, wildcard characters are used to avoid listing all the different singular and plural word forms.)

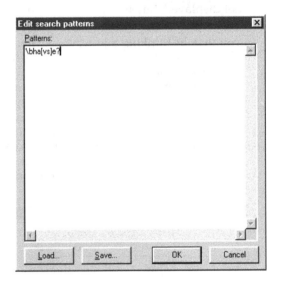

Figure 34: Entering search patterns in a Batch Search

save/load As mentioned above, complex searches can be saved to a file or loaded from a saved file. Let return to our search—based on a regular expression—for the English present perfect tense with an optional adverbial or negative in it. That search query was formulated as
\bha[vs]e?(\W\w+){0,1}\W\w\w\w\w+e[nd]\b. We can use BATCH SEARCH to save this search query to a file. We select BATCH SEARCH in the ADVANCED SEARCH dialogue box which leads to the appearance of the three buttons related to the kind of search: EDIT PATTERNS, IMPORT PATTERNS and BATCH OPTIONS.

84

As illustrated above, clicking on EDIT PATTERNS brings up a large text box (EDIT SEARCH PATTERNS) in which multiple entries can be entered (on successive lines or separated by commas). Here we enter our search query for the perfect tense and choose SAVE from the options at the bottom of the window. This invokes the usual save file dialogue box and we can then enter a suitable filename for this search term. Once the search query has been saved, we can retrieve it at any time by choosing BATCH SEARCH and selecting IMPORT PATTERNS, which will allow the loading of the search file.

One important feature of BATCH SEARCH is the fact that it can be used with any of the three search types. Here we are combining a BATCH SEARCH with a REGULAR EXPRESSION search.

Let us continue with our search query based on the present perfect and look at the way in which the search results (rather than the search query itself) can be saved directly to a file. Clicking on the SAVE TO FILE checkbox found under the BATCH SEARCH checkbox, causes two buttons to become accessible: BATCH OPTIONS at the top of the dialogue box and SAVE OPTIONS at the bottom, next to SAVE TO FILE.

Clicking on BATCH OPTIONS brings up a BATCH SEARCH options dialogue box (Figure 35), which allows the appropriate format of the saved results file to be specified. On the right are the suppress options. As usual, up to two out of the three data structures in the corpus (TAGS, PART OF SPEECH, and WORDS) can be suppressed in the output. Two buttons, CONTEXT TYPE and SORTING, on the left of the dialogue box allow further control over the form of the saved output. The CONTEXT TYPE button reveals the usual choices—characters, words, lines and sentence—and the SORTING button contains the ADVANCED SORT options. (See Section 11.2.) Performing a BATCH SEARCH and saving the results to a file is actually much more straightforward than the long description of options presented here might suggest.

When all the options have been fixed, clicking the OK button in the ADVANCED SEARCH dialogue box prompts the user for the filename to be used to store the results. Once the filename is entered and SAVE selected, the search starts. No hits are displayed on the screen, but it is possible to track the number of hits found and to view the progress of the search through the corpus, When the corpus has been completely searched (or when the user selects CANCEL), the results are processed and saved to the appropriate file. Naturally, the search can take some time and the resulting files may be quite large.

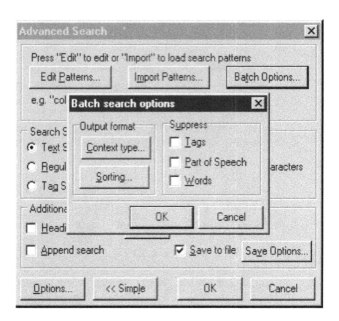

Figure 35: Saving the results of a Batch Search to a file

In general, it is a good idea to use the BATCH SEARCH option for complex searches that are to be performed several times.

8.2 Context search I

@ range

It is possible to search for *speak* followed by *mind* two words to the right by using a simple TEXT SEARCH and searching for **speak * mind**. This is an example of a context search, which is more restrictive than a regular search. We are searching for *speak* with a right context of "a word followed by *mind*." The obvious limitation here is that the context must be stated in terms of a set or known number of words to the right. What we want to be able to specify is a range of intervening words. This is accomplished by using the wildcard @, which we have already seen in action above. The range matched by @ is set within the SEARCH OPTIONS dialogue box and can be anything from 0 (no intervening words) to 9 (nine intervening words). Thus we can search for strings using the format **speak @ mind** (or **speak@mind**), with the value of @ set to a range such as 1-3, 2-4, etc. If it is necessary to search for @, i.e., treat it as a literal symbol, then any alternative symbol, such as #, can be entered as the new range wildcard in SEARCH OPTIONS.

Some additional points: It does not make any sense to start or end a search query with @, and an error message will occur if you try to do this. On the other hand, there is no limit to the number of times @ can be used in a search, and as we have seen, the wildcard @ can be used in both simple text searches and in tag searches. This range symbol cannot be used in regular expression searches, however.

8.3 Context search II

A left and a right context can be specified by checking the HEADINGS/CONTEXTS box under ADDITIONAL SEARCH CONTROL in the ADVANCED SEARCH dialogue box. Selecting EDIT brings up a dialogue box in which contexts restricting a search can be specified. The left and right contexts may be tags or mark-up such as <TITLE> and </TITLE> or plain words and phrases.

Note: Setting the left context as > and the right context as < is one way to ignore the html tags when searching a web-page.

Let us look at a made up "fruit" text to see how this works. The potential targets of the search are the variations on **word** (in boldface), and the underlined <u>fruit</u> words are potential contexts, used here for illustrative purposes.

word mmm <u>apple</u> mmmmm **worda** mm m mmm <u>banana</u> mmmm m mm mm **wordb** mmmmm mmm mm mm **wordc** mmm mm mm **wordd** mm mm <u>plum</u> mmmmm mmm mm. mmm **worde** mm mm m mmm <u>apple</u> mmmm **wordf** mm mm <u>banana</u> mmm **wordg** mmm <u>apple</u> mmmm mmm <u>banana</u> mmm <u>plum</u> mmmm **wordh**.

First of all, as a baseline, note that if we perform a simple (non-context) search for **word%** (where % is a wildcard character), we will find all nine instances. On the other hand, if we perform a context search in which the left context is specified as **banana**, then the search will pick up *wordb* to *wordh* — that is, all the instances except the first two, which both occur before *banana*.

Adding **plum** as a right context changes the procedure as follows: The search algorithm works though the text until it finds the left context (**banana**) and then starts searching for all instances of *word%* until it encounters the right context (**plum**). Once the right context word is found, the program continues to run through the text looking for the left context again before registering any further instances of *word%*. Thus specifying a left context of **banana** and a right context of **plum**, the program will locate *wordb, wordc, wordd,* and *wordg*.

If you try a sample search like this and don't get the expected results, you should make sure that (i) the HEADINGS/CONTEXT box is selected and (ii) the appropriate search settings are selected (such as IGNORE CASE OF LETTERS).

Is this clear so far? If not, you should step through the above searches using the "fruit" text to convince yourself that the search results will indeed turn out as stated. You might work through the fruit text and write ON when the left context is reached and OFF when the right context is located, then look for the search terms located between ON and OFF. Alternatively, you should create your own toy text and try out various possibilities.

We can make the left context more complex and use the "phrase" **mm banana**, keeping **plum** as the right context. What will the program find now? Only one instance of *word%*, namely *wordg*.

@@ long range What if we want to allow discontinuous elements in the left context, say *banana* followed somewhere in the text by *apple*. To achieve this, we use the extended range character @@. With the left context specified as **banana@@apple** and the right context as **plum**, a search for *word%* would finds *wordf* and *wordg*, We can also use @@ in the right context. We can illustrate this using our dummy text once more. Imagine that we set the left context to **apple** and the right context to **banana@@plum**. The first instance of *word%* to be found is *worda*. Next the beginning of the right context (*banana*) is encountered and the search for *word%* is suspended as the program ploughs through the text looking for *plum*. Once *plum* is located, the program searches for the left context *apple* again and after processing the whole text the end result is that two items *worda* and *wordf* are found.

A minor point: The results of searches in which the left context is X and the right context is Y@@Z are very similar to searches in which the left context is X and the right context is simply Y. Differences occur when an X occurs between Y and Z. Such specifications may not give the result expected by the user because a left context may be ignored because it is in the scope of @@ in the right context.

There is nothing to prevent the use of the same word as both a context and a search term, except, of course, rampant confusion in the mind of the user.

Having worked through the basic mechanisms using the "fruit" text, you might try a context search in a real text before reading further details about context-constrained searching.

regex context The above explanation of context searches is based on the use of simple text searches, but it is also possible to combine a context search with a REGULAR EXPRESSION search. Selecting this search option means that **both the search query and the context will be interpreted as regular expressions**. Taking of advantage of the flexibility that regular expression syntax allows us, we can use disjunctions (among other possibilities) in identifying the context strings. For example, we can specify the left context as **apple | banana** (or **app | ban**).

tag context It will now come as no surprise to learn that it is also possible to add context restrictions to a TAG SEARCH so that specifications using the word&tag format can be entered as left and right contexts. It is also possible to use the long range wildcard @@ in the context specification.

With all these searches the main thing to remember is that the syntax appropriate for the specification of the left and right contexts is the same as the syntax of the search query, with the proviso that @@ is only meaningful in the specifications of contexts and cannot be used in the search query.

left vs. right Finally, we should note that it is permissible to specify only a left context with no right context, but not to set a right context with no left context.

8.4 Heading search

select texts Some corpora (such as the *British National Corpus*) are structured in such a way that they are divided into a series of headings and texts. The heading, which contains information about a text, is followed by the text itself. The HEADING SEARCH enables the user to select which texts are to be searched, based on the presence of particular specifications in the heading. Thus if the headings contain an annotation about the sex of the authors, then it should be possible to search only those texts written by female authors. For example, the pattern entered in the heading search might be **author=fem**.

To perform a heading search, you first check the HEADINGS / CONTEXTS box (towards the bottom of the ADVANCED SEARCH dialogue box) and then choose EDIT. In the HEADINGS / CONTEXTS search dialogue box that arises, choose EDIT again. A HEADINGS CONFIGURATION dialogue box appears in which you can ADD (i) a heading name, (ii) the begin and end tags that delimit the heading, and (iii) the tags that indicate the beginning and ending of the text itself.

Once the HEADINGS CONFIGURATION has been specified, the PATTERN to be searched for in the heading (e.g., **author=fem**) can be entered in the HEADINGS / CONTEXTS search dialogue box. All the heading information is now in place and so it just remains to enter the search query itself.

This is another kind of context search. It allows us to search for a word (say *victory*) used in texts written by female authors. Once the headings have been specified as above, a search can be initiated. The program locates the heading and looks for the pattern specified (e.g., **author=fem**). If the pattern is found, then the text following the heading is searched for the string specified in the search text box (e.g., **victory**). If the pattern author=fem is not found in the header, then the program ignores the corresponding body of text and checks the next header for the presence of author=fem, and so on until the entire corpus has been searched.

8.5 Append search

combination
You may sometimes wish to combine the results of two searches. For example, if you wish to approximate a lemma search for GO, you might search for **go%%**, and then perform an APPEND SEARCH for **going,** and then another APPEND SEARCH for **went.**

To do this, you perform the first search, then check APPEND SEARCH in the ADVANCED SEARCH dialogue box. This leads to the concordance results from the second search being appended to the end of the concordance lines from the first search.

As noted above, a REGULAR EXPRESSION search can used to achieve the same results much more efficiently, but the APPEND SEARCH option is conceptually simpler.

X no Y
An APPEND SEARCH is useful when a first search is restrictive and a second search will add some additional results. For example, say that you want to look for all instances of *way* except those are preceded by the word *no*. One way to do this is to use the following regular expression query: **\b[a-mo-zA-MO-Z]\w*\Wway\b.** This search omits all instances of *no way*, but in fact omits all words beginning with *n* that occur with *way*. To restore some of these lost instances, we could do an APPEND SEARCH for **\b[nN]\w\w+\Wway\b,** which finds all n/N-initial words longer than 2 letters occurring before *way*.

In truth, this search could be done in one pass using a disjunctive REGULAR EXPRESSION search:
\b[a-mo-zA-MO-Z]\w*\Wway\b | \b[nN]\w\w+\Wway\b
(or alternatively, **(\b[nN]\w\w+ | \b[a-mo-zA-MO-Z]\w*)\Wway\b**) but the APPEND SEARCH does have the advantage of making it easier to check that each component of the search is doing what is expected.

9. General Search Control and Options

customisation The parameters controlling searches are located in two places: GENERAL SEARCH CONTROL in the ADVANCED SEARCH dialogue box and in SEARCH OPTIONS.

The features under GENERAL SEARCH CONTROL (visible in Figures 28, and 29) are checkboxes for:

IGNORE CASE OF CHARACTERS

USE SKIPPING AND EQUAL CHARACTERS

SENTENCE MODE

The features under SEARCH OPTIONS (shown in Figure 19) are:

MAX SEARCH HITS

FREQUENCY OF HITS

CONTEXT TYPE

Special characters

    Range character

    TAG SEARCH SEPARATOR

    CHARACTERS TO TREAT AS (word) DELIMITERS

    SKIPPING CHARACTERS

    EQUAL CHARACTERS

Wildcard characters

HEADINGS

9.1 Ignore case of letters

The "factory" default is set such that searches that are insensitive to case, that is, a search for **let** will find *Let* and *LET*. To change this setting, simply check (or uncheck) the box labelled IGNORE CASE OF LETTERS in GENERAL SEARCH CONTROL.

case and [a-z] This setting can have wider ramifications than you might expect. For example, a REGULAR EXPRESSION search for **[A-Z]** will (surprisingly) match a lower case letter if IGNORE CASE OF

91

LETTERS is selected. In addition, the specification in the left and right contexts of context searches is sensitive to this setting, as is the specification of tags in TAG SEARCH.

9.2 Skipping and equal characters

skipp=ing

Selecting the USE SKIPPING AND EQUAL CHARACTERS option by checking the appropriate box in the ADVANCED SEARCH dialogue box brings into force the settings for these two parameters as entered in SEARCH OPTIONS.

The skipping characters are useful for avoiding potential problems with mark-up symbols. It is often the case that words in spoken corpora contain non-alphanumeric symbols that are used to indicate prosodic information. Thus, you may come across different forms of the same word in a spoken corpus: *speaking* and *speak^ing*, for example. This causes a fundamental problem for word searches since a search for **speaking** will miss *speak^ing*. The answer, not surprisingly, is skipping characters. We simply enter ^ in the text box for skipping characters in the SEARCH OPTIONS dialogue box. The result is that a search for **speaking** will find both *speaking* and *speak^ing* (or even *s^p^e^a^k^i^n^g*). Basically, the occurrence of ^ is ignored.

d=t

The EQUAL CHARACTERS option is useful for finding alternative spellings, e.g., making *d* equivalent to *t* (d=t) or for ignoring certain distinctions. Thus if you wanted to disregard the particulars of vowels in a romanised version of Arabic, you could enter a=u=i in the EQUAL CHARACTERS box in SEARCH OPTIONS. If two sets of options are required, they should be separated by a semicolon: d=t; a=u=i.

9.3 Sentence mode

A search for a phrase, particularly a search using the range wildcard character @, may catch words spread across a sentence boundary with the result that the beginning of the string is in one sentence and the end is in the following sentence. Sometimes this is fine, but nine times out of ten, the user will simply eliminate these examples because they do not fit the desired target pattern. Checking the SENTENCE MODE option in the ADVANCED SEARCH dialogue box restricts the search such that hits are only displayed if all the components of the search string occur within a single sentence.

9.4 Maximum number of hits

The maximum number of concordance lines or hits is constrained by various program limitations. The maximum number of concordance lines that can be displayed is no longer limited to 16,000 and so the number of hits can be set to a higher number. However, you may occasionally wish to fix the number of hits. For example, if you are performing several searches, you might want to limit each search to 100 hits, for example.

The factory default setting for the maximum number of hits is 500.

9.5 Frequency of hits

every nth hit The default value for FREQUENCY OF HITS is 1, which means that every instance of the search term found in the text is displayed in the concordance results window. This is usually what you want, but if you search for a very common word, you may well prefer to gather examples from all the files in your corpus, and not just from the first file that is searched. To allow the sampling of hits from a range of text files, you need to change the value of FREQUENCY OF HITS to a larger number. For instance, entering 5 in FREQUENCY OF HITS in the SEARCH OPTIONS dialog box will result in every 5th hit being displayed.

9.6 Changing context type and size

char/word/line Generally, the context is set so that each context line fills the width of the screen, allowing the results to be viewed easily. This is the traditional KWIC display. However, there are, in total, four context types: characters, words, lines, and sentences, as shown in Figure 36. In addition, for all the options apart from sentence, an appropriate size of context can be specified in the relevant units: 40 characters, 8 words, 2 lines etc.

In fact, there are actually two ways in which the context can be set. First of all, the default context type, which controls the way in which the results of each search are initially displayed is set in SEARCH OPTIONS. The same range of settings also appears in CONTEXT TYPE in the DISPLAY menu. Changing the options in the DISPLAY menu only alters the format of the current results window; it does not change the default setting.

Typically, the default context is based on a number of characters or words. This provides a KWIC display, which makes it easy to visually scan the results. Once the appropriate results have been identified, users may want to switch to a sentence context so that the examples can be saved to a file in the form of a series of sentences.

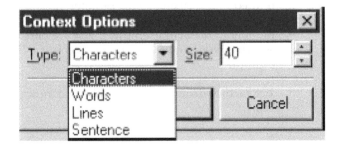

Figure 36: Setting the context for the concordance results

9.7 What is a word?

It is clear that a prerequisite for a word searching program is a definition of what a word is. This is not a particularly difficult issue in written texts—the first definition of a word that comes to mind is a string of letters (and perhaps numbers) surrounded by spaces. And with a little further thought, we would realise that we need to include punctuation symbols, in addition to spaces, as possible delimiters of words. Hence, we can define a word as a string of characters bounded by either spaces or punctuation (plus special computer characters such as the carriage return).

/.:+word\#'{- Let's examine a couple of situations in order to illustrate the subtleties that you are likely to encounter after a little experimentation with concordance searches. To exemplify the complications you might run into, we can consider the first word in the previous sentence. But what is the first word? According to our preliminary definition it is *let*, and the second word is *s*. Similarly, we can ask whether *committee's* should be treated as one word or two. And the same question can be asked concerning *mid-day*, and so on.

MP 2.2 is initially configured so that by default the apostrophe is taken to be part of a word. This means that a search for *let* will not find *let's* because the latter would count as a 5-character word, whereas the search was for the 3-character word *let*. (To find both *let's* and *let*, we would need to specify the search term **let%%**.) If, on the other hand, the apostrophe counted as a word delimiter, then searching for **let** would find *let's* or at least the first part of *let's*.

The advantage of having the apostrophe be part of a word and not a punctuation character (or word delimiter) is that you can then search for the apostrophe. Thus the search *'s would find all possessives, as well as contractions of *is* and *has*. (Note: If

94

you are really interested in possessives in English and want to avoid forms such as *he's* and *it's*, you can ensure that the string before the possessive is at least three characters long by using the search query **???*'s**.)

If you decide that you want to change the search parameters so that *let's* and *let* would both be found by a search for **let**, then you simply select SEARCH OPTIONS and add the apostrophe to the characters that define a word boundary. These characters, the word delimiters, are listed in a text box, and characters can be added or removed from the list by simply typing in or deleting the appropriate characters. In this case, we need to click in the text box and type in the apostrophe character.

error message   Having made this change, we can now search for **let** and find *let's*. On the other hand, a search for **???*'s** will now cause an error message to be displayed, because it is not possible include a delimiter character in a search. (Space is an exception to this rule. It is, of course, possible to include a space in the search string and space will then match any delimiter.)

Let's run through a couple more examples. If you wish to search for sentence boundaries, you can remove "." from the list of delimiters and search for ***.** (Don't make the mistake of searching for **.** alone. This would only work if there were a space between the last word in the sentence and the full stop.) Along similar lines, you might be interested in examining sentence-initial occurrences of a word such as *first*. In this case, you can search for ***. First** (assuming that there are no tags indicating a sentence boundary). And, a sentence-initial active participle may be captured with ***. *ing**.

factory setting   Clicking on the drop down arrow at the end of the delimiter box will reveal a list of previous settings for word delimiters. Any of these previous settings can be restored if necessary. It is also possible to restore the original "factory" setting for the list of word delimiters by selecting the button REVERT TO DEFAULT in the SEARCH OPTIONS dialogue box.

9.8 Changing the wildcard characters

search for %   In discussing search options above, we saw the usefulness of % as a wildcard character. But what if we want to search for % as a literal in *100%*? To allow a search for %, it is necessary to first replace % as a wildcard symbol, perhaps with $, so that %, as %, can be searched for. To do this, select SEARCH OPTIONS and simply substitute $ in the 'zero or one character box' in the SEARCH OPTIONS dialogue box. We can then search for % with the character then being treated literally as a percent sign rather than as a wildcard character.

95

The other wildcard characters ? (exactly 1 character) and * (0 or more characters) and the range character @ can be replaced in the same way. It is also possible to change the word-tag delimiter (&) used in tag searches.

9.9 Headings

Before a heading search can be performed, it is necessary to specify the tags that define the heading and the body. The dialogue box to do this can be accessed from SEARCH OPTIONS or via EDIT in the HEADINGS/CONTEXTS SEARCH dialogue box. (See Section 8.4.)

10. Displaying the Results

10.1 Navigation

Changing from one window to another is accomplished by selecting the desired window from the list in the WINDOW menu. If the CASCADE option in the WINDOW menu is selected, you can simply click on the visible portion of the window you wish to bring to the foreground.

10.2 Change Font, Highlight Font, etc,

large fonts

To change the font, font style, font size, or font colour, select FONT from the DISPLAY menu, then choose CHANGE FONT, CHANGE HIGHLIGHT FONT or CHANGE COLLOCATE FONT. The system font can be changed using the LANGUAGE command in the FILE menu.

10.3 Hide keyword and hide collocates

exercises

In preparing concordance-based exercise materials, it is sometimes useful to hide the keyword. Choosing CONCEAL HITS from the DISPLAY menu results in the keyword (or keywords) being replaced by a dashed line of fixed length.

see vs. watch

Let us look at an example. Say that we wish to prepare an assignment based on the contrast between *see* and *watch*. First, set the FREQUENCY OF HITS to 100 to get a reasonable spread of examples and set the MAXIMUM NUMBER OF HITS to 20 on the assumption that we can get between 5 and 10 good examples from these. Execute a search for *see*, then set the MAXIMUM NUMBER OF HITS to 40, and carry out an APPEND SEARCH for *watch*. We can edit the results and select the best instances of *see* and *watch*, then sort the results to mix the two forms. Finally, we choose the sentence context type, and select CONCEAL HITS. The results can then be saved or printed for use as a reconstruction exercise based on authentic sentences for ESL/EFL students.

97

1. Go home and _____ basketball.
2. I _____ no reason why we shouldn't pursue it.
3. I _____ nothing in the report that tells me what an intellectual climate is.
4. It's interesting that they _____ as much television.
5. It was just embarrassing to _____ it.
6. We have to _____ out for things like that.
7. Now I need to _____ this for a moment just to see if we get on the net here.

Similar exercises can be created based on a single search word. Here is a quick test. Look at the following five concordance lines and identify the concealed word that fits in all the gaps in the following five concordance lines.

____ ?

1. ... thing to remind you of today, ____ this is a public meeting...
2. ... table and introduce ourselves, ____ we're going to be working...
3. ... that may be a thing, actually, ____ it's on the list that we ...
4. ... here for the tail-end of things, ____ I have a 5:00 meeting
5. ... So I think that ____ it's going to be so high ...

It is also possible to hide the collocates by selecting the CONCEAL COLLOCATES command from the DISPLAY menu.

10.4 Word Wrap

The display of text in the corpus file and in the concordance results (if the context type line or sentence is selected) can be controlled by the WORD WRAP command in the CORPUS TEXT menu and in the DISPLAY menu.

10.5 Context Window Size

The relative dimensions of the context window and the concordance results window can be altered by using the mouse to move the boundary between the two in the desired direction. (The mouse button must be depressed when selecting the boundary in order to move it.)

10.6 Suppress words/tags

different views The concordance lines (or corpus) can be "cleaned up" by selecting SUPPRESS from the DISPLAY menu. The choices for suppression are TAGS, PART OF SPEECH and WORDS. Selecting one of these will suppress/display the appearance of the corresponding data structure. Any two of the three data structures can be suppressed at a time.

The form of the tags is specified in TAG SETTINGS in the FILE menu and the program uses this information to hide the tags.

10.7 Distribution

skewed data

It is often useful to obtain a sense of the distribution of hits through a corpus. You might want to check for major skewing in the distribution of hits that might be due to an idiosyncratic file or to the different sub-corpora that are present.

Selecting DISTRIBUTION in the DISPLAY menu leads to a graphical display of hits through the corpus or through an individual file. (Choosing DISTRIBUTION will invoke the COLLECT TAG INFORMATION process if it has not been run earlier.)

Warning: If the concordance results window is not active, then the DISTRIBUTION command will not appear.

The graph in Figure 37 shows the distribution of *speak* in the Meetings sub-corpus. The x axis indicates the number of hits and the y axis shows the position in the corpus (or in a particular file). If the PERCENT checkbox is deselected, the y axis displays line numbers rather than percentages to indicate position.

The box labelled SCOPE at the top of the screen allows the user to toggle between a display of hits in the entire corpus and the hits in a single file.

In the chart below, we see that there are 11 instances of *speak* in the first 10% of the corpus, and 12 instances in the second 10%. (Selecting LABELS leads to the display of the number of hits for each row.) One use of the overall distribution pattern is to highlight areas of the text in which a particularly high or low frequency of *speak* occurs.

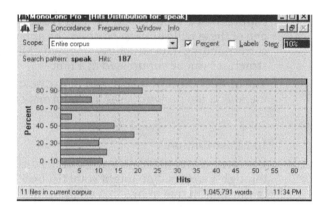

Figure 37: The distribution of "hits"

In the graph shown, the number of hits are calculated for each 10% of the corpus. Other divisions of the corpus (or file), segments comprising 2%, 5%, 20%, 25%, 33% and 50%, can be set (in STEP at the top of the window).

The graph in Figure 38 shows the distribution of *just* in five files in the Meetings sub-corpus. The x axis indicates the number of hits and the y axis shows the individual files name.

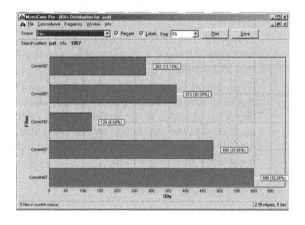

Figure 38: Distribution of hits in individual files

To print a copy of the table, click on the PRINT button at the top right of the window (visible in Figure 38).

10.8 Locating hits

tracking info   Selecting a line in the concordance results window invokes the display of information about the source of the hit in the lower

100

left of the screen. The information given includes the file name and—if specified in TAG SETTINGS—page number, line number and tracked tags. (See Section 3.2.) This information can also be seen by clicking on the line with the right mouse button (see Figure 39) and choosing DISPLAY INFO.

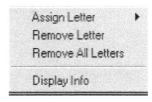

Figure 39: Adding or viewing information associated with a concordance line

A window comes into view, illustrated in Figure 40, that provides information on the source file/page/line and on the value of tracked tags. The specification of tags to be tracked is given in TAG SETTINGS (NORMAL TAGS) in the FILE menu. (See Figure 5.)

10.9 Changing KWIC, Sentence, ...

The form of the context—words, characters, etc.—for the concordance results can be changed via CONTEXT TYPE in the DISPLAY menu. See Section 9.6 for details.

Figure 40: Information relating to a concordance line

101

11. The Power of Sorting

11.1 Sorting

As mentioned above, the search terms in the concordance window are displayed initially in what is referred to as text order. However, much of the utility of a concordance program derives from its ability to re-sort the items in such a way that similar forms line up together. This re-sorting reveals recurrent patterns in the text, as illustrated earlier with the search for *speak*. Once the concordance lines are sorted in an appropriate manner, the user can scroll though the results to visually identify common patterns.

Aggregating similar patterns is accomplished by ordering the concordance lines so that they are alphabetised according to, for example, the word to the right of the search term. This is a 1ST RIGHT sort. Other similar sorting options are 2ND RIGHT, 1ST LEFT, 2ND LEFT, ORIGINAL TEXT ORDER, or SEARCH TERM. Choosing one of these sort orders specifies the primary sort. Once one item is selected from the SORT menu, the mouse can be moved horizontally to select a second sort, which specifies the secondary sort order. The primary and secondary sort orders 1ST RIGHT, 1ST LEFT and 1ST LEFT, 1ST RIGHT are commonly used and hence are listed separately in the SORT menu.

1st R, 1st L   A 1ST RIGHT, 1ST LEFT sort means that the concordance lines are sorted alphabetically according to the word following the search term, and then, if there are lines in which the same word occurs after the search term, these lines are further sorted according to the alphabetical order of the word preceding the search term.

alphabetical   The particular meaning of alphabetical order is determined by Windows (not by the software) and depends on the language setting in place.

11.2 Advanced sort

An ADVANCED SORT option is divided into two parts. The first, upper component of the dialogue box invoked by the selection of ADVANCED SORT allows the user to choose a primary, secondary and tertiary sort order (labelled as FIRST SORT, SECOND SORT and THIRD SORT).

reverse sort In addition, for any sort position a reverse sort can be selected. A reverse sort orders the lines in alphabetical order of the endings of words with the result, that *panda*, for instance, comes before *bear*. (This feature may be especially useful if you are working with Arabic or Hebrew.) The second component is a customised sort, which is selected by a checkbox. This provides even more flexibility since the user can enter a range for the sort, such as 3L-3R. This range will sort the lines 3L, 2L, 1L, SW, 1R, 2R and 3R! Alternatively, the user can specify a sequence of sort domains separated by a comma. The terms permitted in this listing are as follows:

3L, 2L, 1L, 1R, 2R, 3R

0 = Seach term

DEF = Defined sort

ORIG = Original order

1Lr = 1st Left, reverse sort

Note: If the customised sort option is checked, it is impossible to select items such as FIRST SORT, SECOND SORT, etc. in the upper portion of the dialogue box.

11.3 User-defined sort

grouping A further option available under ADVANCED SORT is a DEFINED option. This allows the categorisation and grouping (i.e., sorting) of concordance lines according to user-defined categories. Thus if you have five categories or classifications that are appropriate for a set of concordance results, you can assign the letter *a, b, c, d,* or *e,* as appropriate, to each line. To do this, select (click on) a concordance line, click on the right mouse button and assign a letter to that line. (See Figure 39, page 101.) The assigned letter is then displayed to the left of each concordance line. Choosing the DEFINED option in ADVANCED SORT orders the lines according to the letters assigned by the user, which will group the members of each type together.

A further parameter that can be used to sort the concordance lines is Tracked tags.

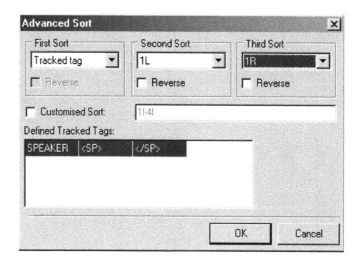

Figure 41: Sorting according the value of a tag

In the example shown above, the First Sort is defined in terms of the value of the Speaker Tag, which means that the concordance lines will be reordered in a way that clusters the hits associated with each speaker.

In this example, there is only a single tracked tag. If there are multiple Tracked tags, the one to be used in sorting can be selected from the DEFINED TRACKED TAGS box.

12. Collocates and Collocations

12.1 Collocate frequencies

MP 2.2 furnishes a variety of frequency statistics, but the two main kinds are corpus frequency and collocate frequency. The command CORPUS FREQUENCY DATA creates a word list for the whole corpus, as described in section 3. Choosing COLLOCATE FREQUENCY DATA from the FREQUENCY menu (or CTRL-F) displays the collocates of the search term ranked in terms of frequency.

frequency
The collocates of a word are its frequent neighbouring words. In *MP* 2.2, the collocate frequency calculations are tied to a particular search word and so the frequency menu only appears once a search has been performed. The collocation data produced by the COLLOCATE FREQUENCY DATA command is typically organised in four columns, with one column for each position surrounding the keyword: 2nd left, 1st left, 1st right and 2nd right. (Thus 1st left refers to the word before the search term and 1st right refers to the word following the search term.) The columns show the collocates in descending order of frequency.

The span of the collocates displayed is set in FREQUENCY OPTIONS. The values are 1L-1R to 4L-R.

Above, we examined the simple question of which words frequently follow *speak*. Once we have searched for *speak*, we can select COLLOCATE FREQUENCY DATA and see at a glance what the common words following *speak* are. The collocates of *speak* (in four positions) are given in Figure 42 and we find, not surprisingly, that *to* is the most common word following *speak*, but we also get a sense of the variety of other common collocates following *speak*. The most frequent left collocate of speak is the infinitival *to*. Remember that we searched for the base form *speak* and the grammatical consequences of this choice can be seen in the words showing up in the 1-Left column. Note the occurrence of *come* as a collocate of *speak* based on the American usage *come speak*. (British English prefers the coordinated structure, *come and speak* over the serial verb construction.)

re-calculate

Note: The COLLOCATE FREQUENCY DATA command can only be chosen when a concordance results window is active. Note also that if you want to force a recalculation of the collocate frequencies, you must first close the COLLOCATE FREQUENCY DATA window. Thus, you must be careful about choosing the COLLOCATE FREQUENCY DATA command after having deleted some concordance lines. If no collocate window tied to the concordance is open, then the collocates will be (re-)calculated and everything will be fine, but if a collocate window already exists, then the COLLOCATE FREQUENCY DATA command will simply bring up the existing collocates window, the contents of which will not reflect the current state of the concordance results.

MonoConc Pro - [Frequency Statistics - [speak]]

File Concordance Frequency Display Window Info

2-Left		1-Left		1-Right		2-Right	
14	want	72	to	58	to	23	the
11	I	11	can	12	with	17	that
10	like	8	we	10	about	14	this
5	Can	8	you	9	up	9	a
5	need	7	would	7	for	7	us
5	you	5	I	7	in	5	it
5	opportunity	5	don't	6	a	5	and
5	we	4	will	5	against	5	you
4	to	4	and	4	Spanish	4	my
4	come	4	come	4	into	4	to
4	can	3	didn't	4	on	3	I
4	that	3	me	3	the	3	some
3	wants	3	can't	3	from	3	language
3	who	3	just	3	as	3	is

1,090,460 words   06:11

*Figure 42: Collocate frequency table for **speak***

The calculations involved, especially for the corpus frequency counts, require a fair amount of computation and may take some time. In addition, there is also a limit to the amount of data that can be held in display window. (See BATCH FREQUENCY, Section 5.3, for an alternative that directs the results to a file rather than the usual window display.)

Firth

The usefulness of collocate frequencies in providing information of various kinds should not be underestimated. The linguist J.R. Firth is often quoted as saying that you shall

108

know a word by the company it keeps. The ramifications of this statement made in the 1950s are still being explored today. (See, for example, *Text and Corpus Analysis* by Michael Stubbs, *Patterns and Meanings* by Alan Partington and *Corpus Collocation Concordance* by John Sinclair.) Corpus analysts tend, in one way or another, to explore the extent to which the formal and semantic properties of a word are reflected in its collocates.

Let's look briefly at a simple investigation to explore the role of collocations as a guide to meaning. The words *wide* and *broad* will suffice as an example of a pair of words that can be described as synonymous. Synonyms, words having the same meaning, might reasonably be expected to show up with the same collocates since these would be equally compatible with either of the synonyms. On the other hand, differences in the range and frequency of collocates occurring with each of the two synonyms may be used to provide clues to subtle differences in meaning. An examination of the set of collocates of a word provides some evidence about meaning, a domain that is generally agreed to be difficult to investigate and for which it is hard to find any empirical data.

We can perform searches for *broad* and *wide* and examine the collocates of each word. The most frequent left and right collocates of *broad* and *wide* in the *BNC Sampler* corpus are given in Figures 43 and 44.

No.	1-Left	No.	1-Right
23	*a*	5	*Street*
13	*the*	3	*search*
10	*in*	3	*and*
2	*and*	2	*as*
2	*as*	2	*categories*
2	*very*	2	*leaved*
2	*these*	2	*smile*
1	*large*	2	*dispersal*
3	*to*	2	*based*
1	*of*	2	*range*
1	*for*	2	*church*
1	*his*	2	*daylight*

Figure 43: Left and right collocates of **broad**

109

No.	1-Left	No.	1-Right
49	*a*	20	*range*
10	*the*	14	*ranging*
7	*inches*	10	*and*
6	*world*	9	*variety*
6	*and*	6	*open*
6	*enterprise*	5	*client*
5	*metres*	5	*area*
5	*in*	4	*of*
3	*open*	3	*Open*
3	*is*	2	*mouthed*
3	*very*	2	*implement*
3	*for*	2	*eyed*

Figure 44: Left and right collocates of **wide**

Examining the concordance results from this small sub-corpus, we find that *wide* can have an adverbial, as well as adjectival function with the result that the left collocates of the two words are somewhat different. In addition, *broad* occurs as a proper name (as in *Broad Street*), adding to the complexity of the comparison of the two words.

Comparing the right collocates of the two words, we see that *range* occurs with both *broad* and *wide*, but that other right collocates are not shared by the two words. Examining the words that collocate with only one of the pair of words should provide some clues to the differences in meaning of the two synonyms. Taking this approach, we can omit words such as *range* and just list those right collocates that occur with only one of the synonyms. Here we ignore frequency data and simply compare the two lists of words looking for clues to the nature of the differences between the two synonyms. The first few examples from a list of collocates unique to each word are shown in Figure 45.

A similar approach is to examine the frequent collocates of each synonym and to see whether the collocate also occurs with the other synonym. The sample data in Figure 46, based on a large newspaper corpus, shows ten frequent collocates of *broad* and *wide* and an assessment, based on the corpus, of the potential for each collocate to occur with the other synonym.

broad	wide
alliance	acceptance
answers	alcohol
aperture	appeal
averages	arching
band	area
based	areas
bases	associations
basis	awake
bay	beaches
bean	berth

*Figure 45: Some unique collocates of **broad** and **wide***

broad collocates	collocate of *wide* ?	wide collocates	collocate of *broad* ?
range	yes	range	yes
and	yes	ranging	yes
based	rare	and	yes
Street	yes	of	rare
money	no	open	no
daylight	no	variety	rare
church	rare	Web	no
spread	yes	eyed	no
brush	rare	on	no
beans	no	Fund	no

*Figure 46: Comparison of ten most frequent collocates of **broad** and*
wide

The data in Figures 45 and 46, which has been compiled from concordance and collocation results, not generated directly by the program, can be used to guide a description of the similarities and differences between *broad* and *wide*. One difference, for instance, is that *wide* often describes the horizontal distance between two or more points, while the semantically more restricted *broad* suggests a horizontal distance between two or more positions on a (possibly conceptual) surface.

12.2 Advanced collocations

collocations One disadvantage of the simple collocate frequency table (as shown in Figure 30) is that it is not possible to gauge the frequency of collocations consisting of three or more words. Thus, we cannot tell from the *speak* collocates table how common the phrase *to speak to* is. To calculate the frequency of three word collocations, it is necessary to choose ADVANCED COLLOCATION from the FREQUENCY menu. The top part of the dialogue box associated with ADVANCED COLLOCATION allows the user to choose from up to three word positions and the appropriate choice for *to speak to* would be 1L, Search term, 1R. The program calculates the frequency of the three word *"speak"* collocations based on this pattern.

count The ADVANCED COLLOCATION option can also be used to count the different components making up the search term. The main collocate frequency table always ignores the search term, which means that if you use wildcard characters or tags in the search query and capture a variety of words as hits, then you need a way to count the different words. You can do this by using ADVANCED COLLOCATION and selecting SEARCH TERM in one column and setting the other two columns to NONE. The ADVANCED COLLOCATION routine will then calculate the frequency of each of the search term forms.

The ADVANCED COLLOCATION dialogue box (like ADVANCED SORT) is divided into two sections. The lower part of the dialogue box is labelled Customised Collocation. When checked, this option allows the user to enter word positions (1L,0,1R) defining the collocation into a text box. The user can list positions separated by commas or enter a range of words such as 2L-2R.

One component of ADVANCED COLLOCATION is SPAN, as illustrated in the dialogue box below.

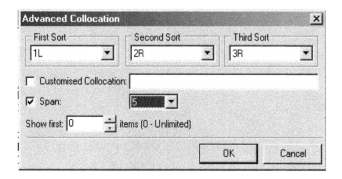

Figure 47: Advanced Collocation dialogue box

The value of span can be set to between two and five words. With the above setting of 5, the program will generate a frequency list of 5-word clusters containing the search word.

The calculation and display of collocations is guided by the settings in FREQUENCY AND COLLOCATION options. See Figure 11.) This dialogue box is invoked by selecting FREQUENCY OPTIONS from the FREQUENCY menu.

12.3 Saving and printing the results

The output from the frequency analyses can be saved to a file by choosing SAVE AS FILE from the FREQUENCY menu. The frequency file that is active—the collocate frequency or the corpus frequency—will be saved to a text file. The frequency results can be printed using CTRL-P or PRINT. Once again, it is the frequency file that is active that will be printed.

13. Working with Languages Other Than English

13.1 File format

The appropriate format for *MP* 2.2 files is ANSI (Windows text). If your non-English files are in ASCII format and you load them into MP 2.2, then the accents may appear garbled. You need to load the files into a Windows word processor such as Word, and then save the files (with a different name) as text files. (It may be necessary to close and reopen the file.)

There is also a version of MonoConc that is unicode-based.

13.2 Entering accented characters

Choosing the appropriate language before loading a corpus helps to make the software work appropriately. Choosing a language will not change the keyboard, however, making it difficult to enter special characters such as *ç* and *é* to give examples from French. In order to make it easy to enter these characters in the search string, a French virtual keyboard must be installed. To do this, select Control Panel under Settings in the Windows Start menu. Click on Keyboard and follow the directions for installing keyboards for different languages. Once installed, you can usually press the ALT key to switch from one keyboard to the next.

Many of the language-related settings of *MP* 2.2 come from Windows, which means that the easiest way to work with Chinese, for example, is to install the program on a computer running the Chinese Windows operating system. Under these circumstances, it may not be necessary to make any other selections. However, different encoding systems Choosing the appropriate language before loading a corpus makes the software work in a more appropriate way.

13.3 Working with collocates

A span of 2L-2R works quite well for English, but the default span for other languages such as French might be better set at 3L-3R.

13.4 Working with Chinese, Japanese, Korean

Chinese, Japanese, Korean, and other two-byte languages which do not use spaces to indicate word boundaries present particular problems for a concordancer, which is a word-based searching program. It is, nevertheless, possible to use *MP2.2* to search CJK texts, sort the results, and obtain some basic colllocational information.

It is important to choose the appropriate language/encoding system before loading the files.

13.4.1 Segmented and non-segmented

In most representations, CJK are displayed without spaces between words and a special segmentation program is needed to add spaces or other indicators of a word boundary in the appropriate places—a process that is not trivial. If the text has been segmented, then the ordinary text search will work, as long as the word boundary indicator is listed in the Word Delimiter textbox.

If the text is not segmented, then the simple text search option cannot be used and searching must be done using the regex search option, which is a part of the ADVANCED SEARCH command. This allows all the instances of the search string in a text to be displayed in a KWIC format, in the usual way.

That is the good news. The bad news is that the absence of word boundaries means that it is impossible to look at the collocates of the search string. The only manipulation of the search results that is possible is a right sort. A left sort will be meaningless in this situation since what is interpreted as a word boundary could be anywhere in the preceding string, although one option is to use the reverse option for a Left Sort in the Advanced Sort command. This will sort the characters based on the character immediately preceding the search string.

13.4.2 Left and Right Sort

The easiest manipulation of the search results a 1st Right, 2nd Right sort. A regular left sort will be meaningless in this situation since what is interpreted as a word boundary could be anywhere in the preceding string which means that the characters appearing immediately before the search term would not show any patterning. However, if a left sort is required, we can use ADVANCED SORT, selecting Left Sort and checking the box for the Reverse option. This option ensures that the ordering is based on the character at the end of the "word" rather than the beginning, thus sorting the results based on the character immediately preceding the search string.

13.4.3 Collocates

Since there are no word boundaries, the collocate frequency cannot be used, but it is possible to obtain some collocate information by the following technique. If we wish to get a sense of the collocates following a particular "word", then in the regex search box we enter the search string followed by two dots (..) for each character, thus the most likely options are CHAR.. and CHAR.... (and of course the wild card characters can precede CHAR if necessary). Next we choose ADVANCED COLLOCATION, selecting search term for the first position and none for the other positions. The result will be a list showing the most frequent collocates.

14. Corpora and Language Learning

14.1 Syllabus design

The design of a language syllabus involves many factors, including the aims of the learners for whom the course is designed, but one important factor is an accurate description of the target language, whether it is American English used in professional settings or technical articles written in German or Business Korean. In practice, a description of the language has typically not been based on actual usage, but on a mixture of tradition and intuition (Tomlinson 1998:87).

The language syllabus has traditionally been structured around the presentation of different grammatical tenses, with the dough of grammatical structures leavened with some language functions such as introductions, apologies, and so on. In the majority of cases, however, neither the structural nor the functional components have been derived from an empirical investigation due to both the approach taken to theoretical linguistics and the tradition of language pedagogy, which has not emphasised language description.

The move from some imagined, idealised notions of the target language to usage-based descriptions raises a host of difficult questions due to the very fact that appropriate target behaviour must be identified. The description of language in use is complex and multi-faceted, but one component that is not used extensively today, but nevertheless has a long history within language teaching is frequency lists, which we will consider briefly. (Information on creating frequency lists in *MP* 2.2 is provided in Section 2.).

14.2 Vocabulary and Word Lists

There are various ways in which the word frequency can be related to language learning. On the one hand we can say that data from COBUILD shows that the 50 most common words make up 36% of written and spoken texts. Or, taking more of a learner's perspective we can say that knowledge of the most frequent 2000 words has been seen as an important threshold in language learning (Laufer 1994, Nation 2001:17). Another estimate is that learners who have control over around 6000 words should be able to understand around 90% of a typical text (Carroll et al 1971, quoted McCarthy 2002:16).

There are a variety of issues that need to be considered and here we will just touch on some of them. In the Corpus of Spoken Professional English, the most frequent 20 words, which are all function words, account for around 30% of the words in the corpus. However, presenting the information this way is misleading, since knowing the 20 words clearly does not mean that the learner will understand 30% of the text. The learner may recognise each of the 20 words in their spelling or pronunciation but not in their different uses. And if we distinguish words which belong to different part-of-speech classes, then we get a rather different picture in which the top 20 twenty words in the corpus make up only 20% rather than 30% of the corpus.

Another important point is that a word list does not distinguish the different meanings of words. The word *and* is in the top ten, but we can ask how many meanings of *and* a learner might be expected to know, receptively or productively.

Thus we need to keep in mind that frequency lists are a rough measure of what students need to know since frequency lists are based on the form of individual words and do not give information of the relative frequency of the different uses or meanings of different words. And we can argue whether frequency or range (a measure of the distribution of a word across samples of text) is the most best measure, but the point remains that simple word frequency information is reasonably easy to acquire either from corpus analysis or from secondary sources and it is an important consideration in the design of course materials.

14.3 Collocations

The orthographic conventions of English and other European languages reinforces the salience of individual words, which, in turn, reinforces a naïve model of language in which knowing a language is equated with knowledge of all the words in that language. A more sophisticated version of this view, and in fact a fairly standard view, is that language consists of a set of basic units, words or morphemes, and a framework, i.e., grammar, which governs the distribution of the words. Whether or not this view holds at some abstract level is a matter for debate, but in terms of the processing of language it is likely that the basic units are units large than the word: collocations or chunks, and it is also likely that mastery of these larger units is a crucial part of language learning.

Language teaching materials tend to be collocation-poor, in part because although native speakers use collocations in their speech and writing when they come to construct sentences and dialogues out of context the language tends to consist of unembellished, skeletal sentences, describing the basics of who did what to whom.

14.4 Teaching materials and usage

Words included in course books may not be particulary frequent; may not be illustrated by the most frequent meaning of the word; and are likely to be used in made-up example sentences in which the typical lexical co-occurrences (such as collocations) are absent. Thus corpus-based materials such as concordance lines with the search word concealed can be a useful supplement to traditional textbooks.

14.5 Materials preparation

Materials writers face a difficult task in understanding the structure and functions of language, deciding what to include in language teaching materials, and choosing how to present the information. It is clear from discussions by material writers about their approaches that their views about the nature of language are based on their intuitions, which have presumably been moulded by exposure to the pedagogic traditions of each the particular language they are working on.

Without corpus data, it is difficult for materials developers not to let idealisations and even prescriptivism creep in, and it appears that materials writer rely heavily on their intuition when writing textbooks

14.6 Grammar/vocabulary versus lexis

Most language teaching materials are organised according to a strong grammar vocabulary divide, but corpus research is showing the intimate connections between vocabulary and grammar. As discussed above, lexical links between words, such as between a verb like *find* and its object *a way* which is also likely then to be followed by a purpose clause (to do something). And taking the opposite perspective, we find that grammatical constructions have strong affinities with particular words. Once again corpus-based data can be used to add a lexical dimension to the discussions of grammar in traditional textbooks.

14.7 Learner corpora

As described in Section 2, the construction of corpora needs to be carefully planned. Such planning and attention to data-gathering is all the more important for learner corpora because of the crucial importance of knowledge of the producers since in some sense the loss of contextual information is less important in, say, a newspaper corpus in which the characteristics of the individual writers are less important. In a learner corpus, knowledge of the characteristics of the writer or speaker is crucial, as are the conditions under which the language was produced. Typically, the content of the corpus will be analysed with respect to these features.

A learner corpus is typically an aggregate of the language of several individuals, which can be seen as assessing the language of a class or group of students. Teachers are used to dealing with this kind of assessment and it is enshrined in the notions of levels: advanced beginners. Such an assessment can be used for general planning and for the development of course material and is a part of general pedagogical planning.

To get an understanding of the process of second language acquisition some knowledge of the learning trajectory of individual learners is important. The aggregate view offered by the corpus as a whole is going to mask changes in the language of individuals and hence longitudinal studies are necessary. Practically, this means that an appropriate combination of tagging and retrieval tools is necessary to view the development of language in individuals.

14.8 Learner corpora and pedagogy

Leech (1998:xv) points out the use of learner corpora in providing the teacher with feedback about students command of different aspects of the language, enabling to consolidate what is known and pay attention to areas of difficulty. He also highlights the possibility of comparing the output of students of different first language backgrounds to see what kinds of common problems L2 learners face and what language particular influences occur. Another important factor is the input that the students receive. The students language may well be reflecting the patterns in course materials, which may be reason for some of the unnaturalness in student writing.

A investigation of essay-writing by Lin (2002) showed that *it* was used less frequently by Chinese learners of English than by native speakers, and yet when the different functions of *it* are examined, it turns out that some uses are underused (e.g., tough constructions) and some are overused (dummy *it* in place of dummy *there*).

15. Corpora and Lexicography

In pre-corpus days the ways to create dictionary entries were to rely on the intuitions of the lexicographers or to have some system of collecting and analysing citations, perhaps from classic literature or periodicals. Both citation and corpus approaches are based on usage, in some sense, rather than intuition, but the advantage of using a systematically organised corpus is that you thereby obtain data on different dialects or text types. And it is also possible to get information on frequency and distribution or coverage.

If the aim is to produce a general dictionary of contemporary English or a specialised dictionary, then the challenge is to provide corpora appropriate (and large enough) to meet the lexicographic goals.

15.1 Meaning senses

To work with meaning senses, the concordance lines can be sorted in any way appropriate and then a letter assigned using the list invoked by a right mouse click. The concordance lines can then be sorted according to these assigned letters, using Defined Option in ADVANCED SORT.

15.2 Frequency bands

Both the COBUILD English Dictionary and the COBUILD Learner's Dictionary give frequency information for each word. Words are assigned to different frequency bands, which are indicated by a number of stars. Thus *enthusiasm* is listed as ◆◆◆ and *enthusiastic* as ◆◆. In addition, the senses of each word are listed in frequency order.

We can use the settings in frequency options to produce different frequency bands based on a particular corpus. The number of frequency bands and the way that are composed depend on the aims of the user. Let us assume that we want to simply establish frequency bands in terms of the most frequent 1000 words, the next most frequent 1000 words, and so on.

One way to do this is to produce a frequency list, save it to a file and then use a utility such as Word Count or number paragraphs in Word to identify line 1000, line 2000, etc.

An alternative method is to create the different frequency bands separately. Retrieving the most frequent 1000 words is straightforward and simply depends on adjusting the appropriate parameters in FREQUENCY OPTIONS. The MAXIMUM LINES setting should be 1000 so that we get the top 1000 words, and we need to make sure that MAXIMUM FREQUENCY is set to 0, meaning no maximum. The MINIMUM FREQUENCY can be set to some low number, something like 5 or 2.

The top of the frequency list will look something like Figure 48.

2399703	5.2242%	the
1261891	2.7472%	of
1147127	2.4973%	to
1005529	2.1891%	a
985137	2.1447%	and
790149	1.7202%	in
479240	1.0433%	is
419778	0.9139%	that
404627	0.8809%	for
393817	0.8573%	The

Figure 48: Most frequent words

The information displayed in the last few lines of the frequency list, shown in Figure 49, is important for the creation of the next frequency band, as described below.

5046	0.0110%	tomorrow
5041	0.0110%	particular
5040	0.0110%	growing
5039	0.0110%	cover
5036	0.0110%	born
5024	0.0109%	Clarke

Figure 49: Last items in the 1000-word band

Since we are working with frequency bands, the raw frequency and percentage information is perhaps of less interest to us and so in saving the results to a file, we can choose the "save words only" option. The file can then be manipulated using a word processor or text editor to show the ranking (Figure 50) or to reorder the words in alphabetical order (Figure 51).

1. the
2. of
3. to
4. a
5. and
6. in
7. is
8. that
9. for
10. The

Figure 50: Ranked word list

a
A
able
about
above
according
account
across
action
added
Africa
after
After
again
against

Figure 51: Word list in alphabetical order

We can then create a frequency list for the next 1000 words. Looking at the final, thousandth word in the first list (Fig 49), we have *Clarke*, occurring 5024 times. Since it is possible that other words will occur 5024 times, we need to set the parameters in frequency options in such a way that *Clarke* occurs at the top of the second frequency list Thus we set the that MAXIMUM FREQUENCY to 5024 and MAXIMUM LINES to 1001 so that the *Clarke* entry can be deleted, leaving 1000 items in the list. The top ranked words in the new list, with Clarke ranked first, is shown in Figure 52.

5024	0.0109%	Clarke
5023	0.0109%	spending
5016	0.0109%	poor
5007	0.0109%	subject
5006	0.0109%	areas

5004	0.0109%	contract
5003	0.0109%	provided
4995	0.0109%	common
4984	0.0109%	evening
4983	0.0108%	original
4978	0.0108%	Act

Figure 52: Frequency band for next 1000 words

The lower portion of this second frequency band is shown in Figure 53. Once again this gives information on the MAXIMUM FREQUENCY setting for the retrieval of the next frequency band: 2514.

2522	0.0055%	wonderful
2520	0.0055%	1988
2520	0.0055%	PC
2519	0.0055%	Health
2519	0.0055%	activities
2519	0.0055%	affair
2519	0.0055%	seats
2517	0.0055%	agency
2515	0.0055%	condition
2514	0.0055%	Jonathan

Figure 53: Last items in the 2000-word band

We should emphasise again the issues that come up in producing this kind of word list such as the fact that words are not distinguished according to part of speech. Thus the words *subject* and *contract* in Fig XX, for example, include both verbal and nominal forms.

If you have a corpus tagged with part-of-speech information, you can perhaps obtain a more differentiated frequency list, but it is not at all straightforward since *MP 2.2* is designed to focus on words rather than POS information and some transformation of the text may be needed in order to count the words plus POS tags.

The table in Figure 54 compares the top 20 words in tagged and untagged versions of the same corpus. You can see that common grammatical words such as *to* and *that* are categorised into separate categories in the POS list. Thus prepositional *to* is distinguished from *to* used as an infinitival marker; and *that* as a conjunction is counted separately from *that* used as a demonstrative.

Word-POS Frequency List				Word Frequency List		
101555	3.2886%	the AT		101698	4.7805%	the
46361	1.5013%	to TO		66047	3.1047%	to
45239	1.4649%	of IO		57536	2.7046%	that
40176	1.3010%	I PPIS1		49783	2.3401%	of
36731	1.1894%	and CC		37087	1.7433%	and
36192	1.1720%	that CST		37015	1.7400%	a
36106	1.1692%	a AT1		33740	1.5860%	I
26988	0.8739%	we PPIS2		30011	1.4107%	in
26633	0.8624%	in II		26166	1.2300%	is
26382	0.8543%	is VBZ		22158	1.0416%	you
25628	0.8299%	it PPH1		20884	0.9817%	we
25252	0.8177%	you PPY		19960	0.9383%	it
24314	0.7873%	that DD1		17910	0.8419%	be
18179	0.5887%	's VBZ		17560	0.8254%	have
17900	0.5796%	be VBI		16824	0.7908%	on
17693	0.5729%	to II		15861	0.7456%	this
15818	0.5122%	this DD1		13716	0.6447%	for
14751	0.4777%	on II		13539	0.6364%	And
13531	0.4382%	And CC		13234	0.6221%	think
13265	0.4295%	are VBR		13025	0.6123%	are

Figure 54: Comparison of wordlists with and without POS tags

15.3 Specialised terminology

We can use specialised corpora to produce specialised lexicographic resources. Thus we might analyse a computer news corpus to create a dictionary of computer terms. To accomplish this, we might use the corpus comparison command described in Section 2.

127

16. Linguistic Investigations

Let us look at a simple of example of a how a large corpus might be used to reveal patterns which can then be analysed in traditional ways. We will take *The Times* (of London) newspaper for 1995-1997 (ca. 120 million words of text) as our corpus and use this data to investigate some aspects of the way in which husbands and wives are viewed, at least through the prism of a British newspaper in the mid-nineties.

First, by simply counting the instances of the words *husband* and *wife*, we discover that there are 9,197 instances of the word *husband* and 17,795 instances of *wife*, showing that *wife* is almost twice as frequent as *husband*. Bigamy and polygamy aside, one would expect the number of actual husbands and wives to be equal, and yet there is this large discrepancy, which leads to some interesting questions: To what extent are the newspaper articles about men rather than women, and are women more likely to be referred to via their roles as wives? If women are in fact more likely to be referred to as wives than men are referred to as husbands, then we might expect the phrase *his wife* to occur more often than *her husband* (taking into account the frequency difference in the occurrence of *husband* and *wife*). Looking at the data shown in the table below, we see that this expectation is not borne out. The use of pronouns and articles is remarkably similar for *wife* and *husband*, with about half the instances of *husband/wife* being preceded by *her/his*. On the other hand, there are some differences in percentages, such as the greater percentage of *my husband* compared to *my wife*. Such differences are suggestive and call for closer investigation and a search for explanation.

his wife	48.17%	her husband	49.76%
my wife	8.29%	my husband	10.00%
the wife	7.01%	the husband	6.72%
a wife	2.51%	a husband	3.69%

For further insight, we can examine the words in the corpus that precede *husband*, excluding the grammatical words *my, the,* etc. The result is the following list, which is presented in decreasing order of frequency: *former, first, late, estranged, second, future, new, jealous, dead, violent, devoted, good, drunken, rich, third, French, American, English, elderly, dying, British, faithless, alcoholic, wonderful, unfaithful, daughter's, friend's, philandering, sick,* and *architect.* The equivalent list for *wife* is: *second, first, former, estranged, young, third, new, pregnant, future, farmer's, Minister's, fourth, long-suffering, minister's, leader's, Tory, beautiful, English, divorced, common-law, American, late, battered, vicar's, MP's, political, President's, devoted, doctor's, perfect, French, Blair's, actress, politician's, pretty, good, murdered, non-working,* and *working.*

There are various aspects of these lists that are worthy of comment, both in terms of similarities and differences. One might note the differences in the adjectives used in the two lists: the ones preceding *husband* in many cases refer to negative traits, while the adjectives associated with *wife* are more likely to be either positive traits for a wife, or modifiers portraying the wife as a victim.

Further, we find a notable contrast in these lists between the kinds of possessive nouns that typically occur with each of the two words, as in *daughter's* or *friend's husband* versus *farmer's/Minister's/leader's/MP's/President's/doctor's/Blair's/politici an's wife,* where the possessive nouns preceding *husband* refer to social or familial relations, while those preceding *wife* refer to men in terms of their position or role in society, usually a prominent one.

This brief illustration provides some sense of how something as simple as software that allows the sorting and counting of words in a large corpus can yield new insights and avenues for further investigation into aspects of culture and society, such as the language used to refer to gender and other social categories. Text analysis software cannot provide an automatic interpretation of a text, but what such programs are able to do is transform the text in ways which may provide a fresh and insightful perspective to aid in linguistic or textual analyses.

17. Tricks and Tips: Some Final Comments

As you get used to the different options and settings in *MP* 2.2, you will become more skilled in exploiting different working techniques to manipulate your results in the way that gets as close as possible to the desired goal. In this final chapter, we provide a miscellany of techniques for working with *MP* 2.2.

17.1 Counting the search term

If you perform a search containing some kind of wild card character, then you are like to retrieve different keywords or phrases. Thus a search for *self will find *self* plus *myself, yourself*, etc. How do we then get the program to count the individual instances of the words found? The answer is to use the ADVANCED COLLOCATION command. Choose this command and then set the First Sort to Search Item and the Second and Third Sort Items to None. Click on OK and a count of the different forms of *self* will appear in a results textbox.

17.2 Loading search results as a corpus

There is no save-search feature that allows the retrieval of a concordance results window. The concordance results can only be saved as a file. You might want to recreate a particular concordance window so that, for instance, collocate frequency information can be extracted, and you can do this by loading the saved concordance file as corpus and searching for the search term again.

It may be necessary to adjust the context in order for the concordance lines to display properly and the context window and other links to the original corpus will not be available.

The search term is enclosed in square brackets when it is saved to a text file and it is safest to include the square brackets in the search query (which may involve taking the brackets out of the list of word delimiters in SEARCH OPTIONS).

If you search for the word without the brackets you have to be aware of the possibility of an overcount based on the following scenario. You search initially for a common word such as *thing*. Sometimes *thing* occurs twice in the same sentence, which causes no problem; each instance is displayed on a separate concordance line. If the results are saved with the sentence as the chosen context type, then we have a situation in which the same sentence is included twice, once for each hit. Again this is no problem, but if the saved concordance lines are loaded as a corpus, then there are two extra instances of *thing*. You can delete one of the pair of sentences or you can search for **[[thing]]** and not **thing**. Make sure that you have the same number of hits as you had in the original search.

17.3 Finding hapax legomena

To find all the words that occur only once in a corpus, you simply set both the MINIMUM FREQUENCY and the MAXIMUM FREQUENCY to 1 in FREQUENCY OPTIONS and create a frequency list, which will be displayed in alphabetical order. As always, you should check the word delimiters and the case-sensitive settings to make sure that the results are as required.

17.4 Creating a complete concordance

concordance

One meaning of a concordance is a complete listing of all the words in a text along with their context of use. To achieve this, it would be necessary to find all the words in a corpus and perform a concordance search for each one. *MP 2.2* is a query-driven concordance program and is not designed to produce a complete concordance of a text, but you might approach such a task in the following way. First create an appropriate corpus frequency list; save the list as a file (without the frequency information); modify the list as appropriate (by deleting unwanted words); and then load the file containing the list of words into BATCH SEARCH using IMPORT PATTERNS or using LOAD in the EDIT SEARCH PATTERNS dialogue box.

Note: if you have produced a corpus frequency list, it is best to quit *MP 2.2* before attempting another heavy processing task like this.

17.5 Improving precision of searches

Probably the best way to improve the accuracy of searches is to take the time to master regex searches. Simply using the OR option and the optional character ? in regex searches will make searches more precise.

Other options include using Sentence mode and making searches case-sensitive.

17.6 Extracting collocations

Collocations are tied to search terms and so there is no way to simply extract the collocations in a text. However, if you enter a group of words, such as an academic word list and have the program search for all the terms, you can then use the SPAN option in ADVANCED COLLOCATION to present all the two word (or three word, etc.) collocations in frequency order.

132

EXITING THE PROGRAM

To exit *MP* 2.2, choose EX̲IT (CTRL-Q) from the F̲ILE menu.

APPENDIX 1: REFERENCES

Aijmer, Karin and Bengt Altenberg (eds.) 1991. English Corpus Linguistics: Studies in Honour of Jan Svartik. London: Longman.

Biber, D. 1993. Representativeness in corpus design. *Literary and Linguistic Computing*, 8, 4, 243-257.

Carroll, J.B., P. Davis and B.Richman 1971. *The American Heritage word frequency book*. New York: Houghton Mifflin.

Chafe, Wallace, John W. Du Bois and Sandra A. Thompson. 1991. Towards a new corpus of Spoken American English. In Aijmer, Karin and Bengt Altenberg (eds.) 64-82.

Francis, W. N. and H. Kucera. 1964. *Manual of information to accompany 'A standard sample of present-day edited American English for use with digital computers'* (revised 1979) Providence, Rhode Island: Department of Linguistics, Brown University

Laufer, B. 1994. The lexical profile of second language writing: Does it change over time? *RELC Journal* 25: 21-33.

McCarthy, Michael. 2002. What is an advanced level vocabulary. In Tan (ed.) pp 15-29

Ooi,Vincent B, Y. 1998. *Computer Corpus Lexicography*. Edinburgh Textbooks in Empirical Linguistics. Edinburgh: Edinburgh University Press.

Simpson, R. C., S. L. Briggs, J. Ovens, and J. M. Swales. 2002. *The Michigan Corpus of Academic Spoken English*. Ann Arbor, MI: The Regents of the University of Michigan.

Tan, Melinda. (ed.) 2002. Corpus studies in language education. Bangkok: IELE Press.

INDEX

140